MAKERS OF THE NINETIES
Edited by G. Krishnamurti

HENRY HARLAND

HENRY HARLAND

His Life and Work

by

Karl Beckson

THE EIGHTEEN NINETIES SOCIETY
LONDON · MCMLXXVIII

First published in 1978 by The Eighteen Nineties Society,
28 Carlingford Road, Hampstead, London NW3 1RX, England

Beckson, Karl
    Henry Harland.
    1. Harland, Henry – Biography 2. Novelists,
American – 19th century – Biography
    I. Eighteen Nineties Society
    812'.4   PS1798

ISBN 0-905744-02-0
ISBN 0-905744-06-3 De lux ed.
ISBN 0-905744-01-2 Pbk.

Set in 'Monotype' Caslon series 128 and printed at
The Roundwood Press, Kineton, in the County of Warwick
Made and printed in Great Britain

Contents

Illustrations

Frontispiece   Harland in the late 1880s
[From Edmund Clarence Stedman and Ellen Mackay Hutchinson, eds., *A Library of American Literature*, New Edition, Vol. XI (New York: W. E. Benjamin, 1894).]

between pages 80 & 81

1. Aline Harland, ca. 1890
   [From the E. C. Stedman Papers, Columbia University.]
2. John Lane (in the 1890s)
   [From the E. C. Stedman Papers, Columbia University.]
3. Beardsley Sketch of Harland, ca. 1894
   [From *The Early Works of Aubrey Beardsley* (New York: Dover Publications, 1967).]
4. Beerbohm Caricature of Harland
   [From Max Beerbohm's *Caricature of Twenty-five Gentlemen* (London: Leonard Smithers, 1896); rpt. in *Max's Nineties* (London: Rupert Hart-Davies, 1958).]
5. Henry Harland, ca. 1902
   [From *The Critic* (New York), 44 (Feb., 1940), 108. A studio photograph by Frederick Hollyer, London.]

between pages 96 & 97

6. Harland in 1903
   [From *The Lamp* (New York), 26 n.s. (April, 1903), 227.]
7. Harland's Grave at Yantic Cemetery, Norwich Town, Conn.
   [Photograph by Karl Beckson.]
8. Aline Harland's Grave at Yantic Cemetery, Norwich Town, Conn.
   [Photograph by Karl Beckson.]
9. Ella D'Arcy (in the 1890s)
   [From the E. C. Stedman Papers, Columbia University.]
10. E. C. Stedman (in 1892, aged 59)
    [From the E. C. Stedman Papers, Columbia University.]

Acknowledgements

I am greatly indebted to the countless librarians and assistants in those libraries from which I obtained photocopies of Harland and related material for their cooperation and interest. And to the various curators of manuscript divisions I am indebted for their permission to quote either entire letters or portions of them. In all cases, sources are cited when quotations are given.

In particular, however, I wish to acknowledge the kindness and assistance of the following: Mr Michael Rhodes, Archivist of the John Lane Archive (Allen Lane Foundation) at Westfield College of the University of London, without whose generosity my work would have been more arduous; Albert J. Robbins, of Indiana University, who, as editor of the second edition of *American Literary Manuscripts* (1977), sent me a print-out of locations of Harland letters long before publication of that very useful reference work; Mr Charles Passela, of the Pierpont Morgan Library (New York), who employed an ultra-violet process in order to restore the rare photograph of Aline Harland; Mr Phillip A. Johnson, President Emeritus of the Society of the Founders of Norwich, Conn., who kindly sent me an illustration of Sentry Hill; Mrs Katherine L. Mix, who patiently responded to my many queries with helpful advice; Mrs Eva Reichmann, for her permission to reprint Max Beerbohm's caricature of Harland; Sir Rupert Hart-Davis, for his help in arranging for permission to reprint the Beer-bohm caricature; Mr James Kraft, Executive Editor of the Witter Bynner Foundation, for permission to quote from the Bynner letter to Donald A. Roberts.

Finally, I am indebted to the staff of the Manuscript Division of Columbia University Library for its patience and help in my research among the Stedman Papers. Indeed, without the resources of both the Columbia University Library and the New York Public Library, Astor, Lenox, and Tilden Foundations, my research would have been greatly hampered. To the latter library, I am grateful for its permission to quote extensively from Aline Harland's letters to Richard Watson Gilder in the Manuscript Division and from Henry Harland's letters to Olive Custance in the Henry W. and Albert A. Berg Collection.

CHAPTER ONE

The Early Years (1861-1884)

O N WHAT WOULD have been Henry Harland's forty-fifth birthday, E. C. Stedman, his godfather, wrote to Aline Harland on March 1, 1906: 'His work and name, and the story of what you have been to him and to his genius, will not die.'[1] These, understandably, are words of consolation to a widow. The fact remains, however, that, except for literary scholars of the period, there are few today who have heard of the name of Henry Harland and fewer still who have read any of his works.

Yet the memory of this complex, vital, witty personality remained with his friends and associates as vividly as when he walked the streets of the Cromwell Road in the 1890s. In his memoirs, Richard Le Gallienne recalled Harland as 'one of those Americans in love with Paris, who seem more French than the French themselves, a slim, gesticulating, goateed, snub-nosed lovable figure, smoking innumerable cigarettes as he galvanically pranced about the room, excitedly propounding the *dernier mot* on the build of the short story or the art of prose.'[2] Harland's vitality is magnificently captured by Max Beerbohm in one of his caricatures, but another side of Harland, certainly the more troubled and perhaps the more sinister, is portrayed in Beardsley's sketch of his co-editor of *The Yellow Book*. Arthur Symons sensed this darker side when he later recalled that Harland was 'feverish, a writhing mass of nerves.'[3]

Harland's unlikely background, which he romanticized and mythologized in keeping with his self-created image as a Bohemian, dandy, and wit, was, to his everlasting regret, more prosaic than he could tolerate. Several highly respected encyclopaedias and biographical reference works continue to give his birthplace as St. Petersburg, Russia (a fiction that he himself created, in deference to Whistler, another American *émigré* and poseur who also adopted that exotic birthplace). Harland, however, was apparently born in Brooklyn on March 1, 1861. The only source of information concerning his place of birth is a letter written by a friend, the poet Witter Bynner, who informed Donald A. Roberts (then writing a Master's essay at Columbia University) that he and Harland were both born in Brooklyn.[4] Records of birth for that year have been lost or destroyed; hence, no documentation is possible.[5] In the more reliable biographical accounts, references to Harland's birthplace as New York City overlook the fact that Brooklyn in 1861 was a separate city with its own mayor (it became part of New York City in 1898).

Harland's great grandfather, Thomas Harland (1735-1807), established the American branch of the family when he emigrated from Suffolk County, England, in 1773, to set up shop as a watch and clock-maker in Norwich, Connecticut. Six years later, apparently quite successful (he employed twelve workers and manufactured 200 watches and 40 clocks yearly, as well as jewellery and silverware), Thomas Harland married Hannah Leffingwell Clark and built the ancestral home on Sentry Hill in Norwich Town, adjacent to Norwich. In 1779, the Harlands had a son whom they named Henry (and of whom little is known); in 1822, he married Abigail Leffingwell Hyde, also of Norwich. They had seven children: one was Thomas (named after the successful watchmaker), born in 1830, later the father of the novelist; another was Edward, born in 1832.

In childhood, both brothers had probably known Edmund Clarence Stedman, of Norwich Town, later a prominent member of the American literary establishment and Wall Street broker, who was to play a crucial role in Harland's early literary career. The two Harland brothers and Stedman attended Yale University, but of the three only Edward (or 'Ned,' as he was always called) graduated with a B.A. degree. At Yale, Stedman and Ned were close friends (Tom had attended the university earlier), but Stedman's friendship with Tom later replaced his earlier relationship with Ned. Ned subsequently became a lawyer, then an officer in the Union Army during the Civil War (rising to the rank of brigadier general). With the war's end, he returned to Sentry Hill, where he lived, as a bachelor, with his mother for the remainder of his life.

Before the war, Tom had also become a lawyer, but intellectual restlessness impelled him to seek the vitality of New York, where he often visited Stedman, now married and employed as a clerk for a railway company. Attracted to Bohemian circles of artists and social thinkers, Stedman and Tom Harland made the acquaintance of a radical, Edward F. Underhill, who, following the theories of the eccentric Stephen Pearl Andrews, advocated, in the 1850s, a plan for communal life; he subsequently established 'Unitary Home,' an experimental residence in Stuyvesant Place. Shortly thereafter, four brownstone houses on East 14th Street were purchased to make Unitary Home a permanent residence for the radical group. The Stedmans moved in, and Tom Harland was selected as the home's manager; according to Stedman, Tom's intellect 'dominated the establishment.'[6]

In 1859, Stephen Pearl Andrews, in declining health, came to live at 'Unitary Home,' presumably to continue his life's work on *The Basic Outline of Universology*, eventually published in the 1870s as an 800-page volume, a comprehensive, albeit chaotic, system embracing the basic knowledge of the universe. At the home, a devoted Mrs Jones, who became one of the first women doctors in the United States, nursed Andrews back to health (indeed, he lived for another twenty-seven years) and married him. Mrs Jones's twenty-year-old daughter, Irene, engaged the attention of the preoccupied manager of the home, Tom Harland, who, believed to be 'immune through his quality as a Thinking Machine,'[7] nevertheless succumbed and, following his mentor's example, married the stepdaughter.

Irene Jones, of a Quaker background, had been born in Maine, from where she had been brought to New York. Apart from a family background extending to Pilgrim forebears,[8] little is known of her except that she apparently possessed charm and refinement, that she was devoted to 'Harry' (as he was always called and as he always signed his letters until he settled in England), who, of three children, was the only survivor.

In 1860, Underhill resigned from his position on *The New York Tribune* in order to devote his attention to his position with the Surrogate's Court. Shortly thereafter, Stedman took Underhill's *Tribune* post as a reporter (indeed, Stedman achieved considerable notoriety for his writing on the Civil War). Both Stedman and Tom Harland moved out of 'Unitary Home' at about this time. Why they left is unknown, but possibly growing national dissension that led to the Civil War undermined the Utopian enterprise. With Stedman on the *Tribune*, Harland, despite his lack of journalistic experience, managed to secure a position with the New York *World*. In the following year, Harry (named after his paternal grandfather) was born, and Stedman was chosen as his godfather. Several weeks after Harry's birth, hostilities between North and South erupted at Charleston harbour.

In 1863, Tom left the *World* to accept a position on the

staff of Joseph Lewis, the first Commissioner of the newly formed Internal Revenue Bureau in Washington, D.C., and within three years, he was appointed Deputy Commissioner. Thus, during the Civil War, Tom worked at his desk in the Bureau (and for a time in the Patent Office) in Washington while his brother, Ned, was commanding troops in the field. Irene was with Tom for part of this time, but whether Harry was with them also in Washington is not clear. Two other children, born to the Harlands during the war, died young.[9]

In 1867, Tom Harland returned with his family to New York to become a partner in a legal firm with Daniel G. Rollins, later Surrogate of New York. Settling in Brooklyn in 1871, Tom sent Harry to the Adelphi Academy for four years, then to Grammar School 35, from which he graduated in 1877. Harry spent his summers at Sentry Hill with his grandmother and Uncle Ned, now a prominent politician who represented Norwich in 1869 and in 1878 in the Connecticut legislature. In 1870, he was a state senator and from 1872 to 1876 was a probate judge; in 1883, he served on the Connecticut Board of Pardons while serving as president of a Norwich bank.[10]

At Sentry Hill, Harry was surrounded by a considerable library, of which Margaret Fuller, Stedman's secretary, later wrote: '. . . in Tom and Ed Harland's house on Sentry Hill you can see the books before you mount the stairway. The walls are covered with them.'[11] The cultivated environment of the ancestral home combined with his parents' home in Brooklyn no doubt had a salutary effect upon young Harry. For a while, Stephen Pearl Andrews (still at work on his *Basic Outline of Universology)* lived with his stepdaughter and Tom Harland; perhaps Andrews' reputed knowledge of thirty-two languages had a stimulating effect upon Harry, who early achieved a familiarity with French and Italian.

While Harry was still attending school, a new intellect-tual influence attracted Tom Harland, with a resulting effect upon his son. This was Ethical Culture, whose principal publicist was the German-born son of a rabbi, Felix Adler, responsible for the establishment of the New York Society for Ethical Culture in 1876. Providing a moral force that would be the substitute for what he regarded as a debilitation of religion in the nineteenth century, Adler did not insist on a specific ethical system ; indeed, he did not rule out religious affiliations among the members of the Society. Tom Harland, interested in all forms of intellectual freedom, found this doctrine congenial, for the Harlands attended the Unitarian Church.

According to one writer on Harland, Adler was 'one of Henry's first teachers.'[12] Guided by Adler, the youthful Harry's intellectual interests were turned away from a medical career (he reportedly wished to follow his maternal grandmother, the doctor who had married Stephen Pearl Andrews) ; instead, he became interested in a literary career.[13] Harry's association with Adler and his friendship with an unnamed 'young Jew,' who was a member of the Ethical Culture Society, resulted in a deep interest in 'everything Jewish.'[14] As Harry matured, 'the Jewish element of New York appealed to his imagination, perpetually athirst for picturesque material ; he saturated himself with the romantic traditions of the Jewish race.'[15]

On September 19, 1877, at the age of sixteen, Harry matriculated at the College of the City of New York (now known as The City College of the City University of New York), which, at that time, required five years to complete work for the B.A. degree (the first year, as a 'Sub-Freshman,' was equivalent to secondary school). He took courses in Latin, English grammar, mathematics, history, and freehand drawing, but none in the modern languages. His performance was above the average : at the end of his first year, he ranked 52nd in his class, achieving 3371 points out of a possible 4300.[16] Why he was sent to C.C.N.Y. instead of Yale (which his father had attended and from which his Uncle Ned had graduated) may be explained by at least one fact : the Harlands were living at 249 W. 22nd Street in Manhattan, not far from the red-turreted college located at 23rd Street and Lexington Avenue (and now located in upper Manhattan at 139th Street). Other factors may have been Tom Harland's financial condition and Harry's undistinguished academic record, for City College was a free public institution with low admission standards while Yale, academically superior, was expensive.

Before Harry began his second academic year, the Harlands moved uptown to 35 Beekman Place, at the foot of East 51st Street, where they lived until Tom Harland's death in 1900. Facing the East River and Blackwell's Island (on which there was a prison), now a residential community called Roosevelt Island, Beekman Place was the future setting for Harry's early fiction.[17] The stairs leading down to the bank of the East River, described in his first novel, *As It Was Written*, still exist, but the once quiet bank has been replaced by the incessant roar of the motor traffic on the East River Drive.

By the end of his second academic year, Harry had declined considerably from his class rank in his first year (from 52nd to 107th place), but he was still regarded as a 'good' student, receiving 3024 out of a possible 4400 points : he was 26th in ancient languages, 73rd in natural history, 77th in history, 79th in mathematics, and 105th in drawing.

He was, however, a problem student, for he accumulated many demerits for bad conduct. In his first year, he received forty-one demerits (regarded as unusually high for such a good student), and in his second year, the number rose to an impressive fifty-eight. No records exist to explain the reasons

7

for such a large number of demerits, but perhaps Harry was beginning to be a trifle bored by academic life. He registered for his third year, but no grades are recorded, suggesting that he had left City College between September, 1879, and June, 1880, the precise reason still unknown. What he did until September, 1881, is also unknown. He may have decided to try his hand at writing. It is reported that, in his first year, a classmate in his drawing class asked him, 'What are you going to be when you finish college?' He replied without hesitation, 'I should like to be a poet.'[18] Stedman has written that, before Harland achieved success with his first novel in 1885, he had been writing for several years: 'After suppressing for some years, with my aid, reams of highly imaginative but crude production, he made a continuous success, dating from his first book.'[19]

In September, 1881, Harland registered at the Divinity School of Harvard University as a special student.[20] Whether this resulted from a spiritual crisis in his life is unknown; if so, either it subsided rapidly or he again lost interest in academic study, for, by the end of his first year, he left without a degree or academic credit for work done.

While at Harvard, however, Harland appears to have made an abundance of literary and social contacts in the city of Cambridge. He often went to the home of Mrs A. N. Mosher,[21] where he met such figures as Samuel Longfellow, clergyman and brother of the poet, and William James, Sr., father of two illustrious sons, one of them to be Harland's literary idol. While such intellectual and social discourse no doubt provided stimulation for his literary enthusiasm, Harland was also paying court to the daughters of several households as an 'ardent and whimsical suitor' in Byronic verse.[22] Despite his passionate entreaties, so the story goes, he seems to have adhered to New England proprieties. There is also evidence that, 'despite an unclerical manner in his addresses to the other sex,' Harland preached on at least one occasion in the Bell Street Chapel, Providence, Rhode Island, in March of 1882.[23]

In later years, he fictionalized his year at Harvard, as he did almost every other fact of his life, when talking to journalists. In 1903, on discovering that his interviewer had attended Radcliffe, Harland fabricated a story about attending the University of Paris and Harvard University as an undergraduate :

> As a matter of fact I never was a freshman at Harvard, for I held a B.A. from the University of Paris and so entered Harvard as a sophomore in either '81 or '82. . . . I had been living in Southern France or balmy Italy for years and it is with a shiver even now that I recall how my bright spirit was cabined, cribbed and confined in cold Cambridge throughout those awful winter months. My recollections of Harvard are chiefly of having to get up shortly after midnight to attend some sort of early religious ceremony. . . . I fear I heard also some few professors and wrote down long lists of books, to be consulted subsequent to this lecture, or precedent of the next. But I soon discovered what dreadful old impostors those good professors were ! They did not know a thing that was not in the books beforehand and we would have to read the books and then listen to the professors in the lecture room, telling us just what the books had already said, only with less animation and in inferior diction.[24]

The latter part of this passage indeed has the ring of truth.

In another interview in 1903, Harland seems to have forgotten what he had told the Radcliffe interviewer with respect to the B.A. from the University of Paris, but his remarks about foreign travel may be partially true, accounting for the missing year after leaving City College :

> My father enjoyed going abroad, and since very young, I have been, off and on, in England, Italy, and France.

9

I should not call my father a traveller, he simply liked to go abroad and just went, and I went with him. For this reason, probably, I did not go to school, but had a tutor till I was ready for Harvard. After a year there I went over to Italy.[25]

Harland's need to create a private myth may provide us with a key for an understanding of his complex personality, for such an impulse reveals the need, perhaps, for the reconstruction of an inadequately conceived self. His interest in masks, characteristic of writers associated with the Aesthetic Movement in the late nineteenth century, provided him, as Wilde was later to write in another connection, 'with a method of multiplying [one's] personality' – the artist, in short, conceals the self by revealing it in disguised forms, a method by which he provides himself with freedom of expression. As Wilde's spokesman, Gilbert, states in 'The Critic as Artist': 'Man is least himself when he talks in his own person. Give him a mask, and he will tell you the truth.'[26]

On leaving Harvard in June, 1882, Harland accepted a position as a private tutor of two small boys, spending the summer with them in upstate New York and in the following winter in New York City. One of them, later a distinguished chemist, Frederick G. Zinnser, recalls that Harland was an incessant smoker who read far into the night and who had swings of temperament, from moodiness to gaiety. While the boys did their lessons, he would write but always declined to reveal the nature of his work.[27]

As Albert Parry has stated, Harland had been writing short stories, essays, and novels through his college years and beyond, but 'he could not finish a single *chef d'oeuvre* he set out to write.' Stedman criticised his work, urged him to persevere, and finally advised him to travel in order to broaden his experience. Tom Harland managed to find the money for his twenty-one-year-old son, and, 'with a slender suit-case in his nervous hand,' Harland sailed for Europe early in 1883.[28]

He was away for a year, spending most of his time in Rome among the younger writers and artists, according to Stedman's son, Arthur, who had become Harland's friend and to whom it is unlikely that Harland would invent details. Harland, wrote Arthur Stedman, 'led a delightfully Bohemian existence during the whole period of his stay. His lodgings were in the top floor of the Greek college, one of a series of colleges for the use of foreign theological students in Rome.' During his stay, Harland assisted in editing an English newspaper in Rome, with two Italians, a Greek, and an American ; he also wrote 'a few letters to American newspapers descriptive of Roman life,' but these have never been identified or traced.[29]

Aline Harland has written that by the time her husband had returned from Rome at the end of 1883, 'still scarcely more than a lad, he had found himself. Wholly – in mind and heart – Harland was a Catholic, and he was an artist. However he did not then make his obedience to the Catholic Church. . . .'[30] Back in New York, Harland, without prospects for employment, without vocational training, and without academic credentials, faced a rather bleak future. His father, however, prevailed upon his law partner, Daniel G. Rollins, who was now Surrogate of New York, to provide his son with a position in his office. He was hired as Assistant Accounting Clerk at $100 a month ; in January, 1884, he became Assistant Probate Clerk, and in April, his salary increased by $25 monthly.[31]

As a clerk, Harland was no doubt involved in rather tedious duties, but he apparently did not dislike them, for he never spoke of his position. In his spare time, he continued to labour at his writing. A later novel, *Grandison Mather* (1889), an autobiographical account of what appears to be

Harland's early career as a writer (confirmed by Aline Harland),[32] depicts the writer-hero, Thomas Gardiner, as retiring every evening at seven o'clock, rising 'at the summons of an alarm-clock at two the next morning,' then, 'lighting his lamp and brewing himself a cup of coffee, pegged away at his manuscripts, until the day broke, and it behooved him to get ready to go downtown.'[33] Writing, however, did not always go well, and the memory of those agonizing moments that all writers face is presented in Harland's novel:

> Gardiner would get an idea, a plot, a motive, for an essay, a short story, a novel, an epic, a lyric, and, all aflame with enthusiasm for it, he would sit down to write it out. But conception and execution are two quite dissimilar processes, as everybody knows; one being a sudden, short-lived ecstasy, the other a long, hard, up-hill labor. After he had dashed off a few fervid pages, he would inevitably encounter a stumbling-block, and be brought up with a round turn. Then, while he was casting about for a method of surmounting it, a new idea, a new plot, a new motive, would flash into his head, and cut out the old one, – for in matters of this sort, at any rate, last love is best. And thereupon the half-begun manuscript would be shoved ignominiously into a corner, and an equally brief reign of favor would commence for its successor. You see, he liked nothing better than to build literary castles in the air; but he lacked the patience to toil and moil day after day, until he had forced one of them to materialize in ink on paper. [p. 18]

His inability to complete any of his projected works no doubt contributed to his lack of confidence as a writer. But his life thus far – divided, as it was, between the tedium of the Surrogate's office and his unrewarding attempt to succeed as a novelist – quite unexpectedly took a decisive turn. At the age of twenty-two, Harland fell in love with a bright, intellectual, and artistically gifted young lady (a year older than he), named Aline Herminie Merriam, who lived on East 56th Street, not far from Beekman Place. How they met is unknown, but the romance did not result in a prolonged engagement, for they were married on May 5, 1884, in a religious ceremony performed by the Rev. Theodore C. Williams of East 24th Street.

Like her husband, Aline, on her father's side, had descended from an old New England family, which had emigrated from Kent, England.[34] James Merriam, her father, was a lawyer in New York and possibly an acquaintance of Tom Harland. The fact that the Surrogate of New York, Daniel G. Rollins, was a witness at the wedding may suggest that all three men may have been acquainted professionally. Aline's mother, born in France, had married James Merriam in 1858 (why she was in New York at that time is unknown); her father was in the United States in 1868 as Emperor Louis Napoleon's commissioner to study the American system of education, a study that resulted in major improvements in French schools.

Clearly, Aline Harland, herself an accomplished pianist, had come from a family of considerable attainment. Indeed, Harland's interest in music – and his extensive use of it in his first novel – was no doubt stimulated by his new bride.

CHAPTER TWO

The Mask of 'Sidney Luska' (1885-1889)

ARLAND CONTINUED TO work as a clerk in the Surrogate's office and to write by following his early morning regimen as described in *Grandison Mather*. In a letter dated April 17, 1885, Harland informs Stedman that he has 'just completed' a story, his first novel, of about 50,000 words, filling some 450 manuscript pages, with the title *From Generation to Generation: A Jewish Musician's Story*, combining an interest in the occult, in the sensational, with Jewish characters in New York. He writes to Stedman: 'Though I indulge in one murder, it is on the whole a quiet one and entirely unaccompanied by thunder. . . . The plot is, I think, new ; and the *mise en scène* is among an interesting set of people. No very lofty flights are attempted – simply an unvarnished account by a simple-minded man of a rather curious experience he has had.'[1] Harland was reluctant to have Stedman 'wade through' his manuscript but asked his godfather for advice on how to place it with a publisher. But Stedman, who had become Harland's mentor and unofficial literary agent, read the novel, as he recorded in his diary on May 12, 1885 : 'Have succeeded in placing some of Harland's short stories, but his rude quality & extravagance are ahead of the Amer. market ! He will have to tone down his novel, *From Generation to Generation*, to get a publisher.'[2]

In the April 17th letter to Stedman, Harland raised the

question of publishing his novel under a pseudonym: '. . . would it be very unwise or in very bad taste to publish – provided publication be possible – under a *pseudonym* – and a Jewish pseudonym at that? I think the main semblance of the story would be better carried out if the reader supposed the author to be a Jew.'[3] On the following day, Harland, in another letter to Stedman, explained at greater length why he had decided on a Jewish pseudonym; at the same time, he revealed the extent of his associations with Jews:

> As a postscript to my letter of yesterday I may as well add that one of my reasons for inclining to a Jewish *nom de plume* is an extremely sound one. I know that if a Jew sees the book lying on a bookseller's shelf, and observes that while professing to treat of *Jewish* matters it has been written by so obvious a Gentile as Harry Harland, he will cry, 'Why, what does he know about the Jews?' and drop the presumptuous volume in disgust: whereas, if the Author's name [has] a Jewish flavor, he will on the contrary be disposed in its favor. I have discussed the matter with several Jewish friends, and they concur. How does 'Sidney Luska' strike you? –Another thing, I believe, with a Jewish name on the title page, the sale of the book would be vastly increased. I believe lots of Jews would buy it for that reason, if for no other–for the sake of seeing what New York can produce in the way of a truly Jewish story. I don't think this would be obtaining money under false pretences. For the last six years I have circulated almost exclusively among the Jews, and have thus become all but a Jew myself. I know a good deal more about the Hebrew world of N.Y. than I do about the Xian.[4]

Harland was also convinced that, for the purpose of having the manuscript accepted by a publisher, a Jewish pseudonym would lend authenticity to the work. Thus, he ends his letter to Stedman: 'You know I *am* almost a Jew. So the deception would not be so very black.'

Stedman apparently agreed with Harland on the matter of a Jewish pseudonym, for in an inscription in his first novel, Harland gratefully acknowledged Stedman's symbolic role as godfather in being present at two christenings :

> To Mr Edmund C. Stedman, who twenty-four years ago gave the author a name and a silver cup, and who has since given him a new name and opened for him a golden gate.
>
> 9 September 1885   Sidney Luska[5]

But how had Harland devised such a pseudonym ? According to Louise C. Howe, of Norwich, who knew Harland in later life, the novelist once explained to her that 'my books were about the Jews and every young Jew I had ever heard of was named Sidney, and Luska I thought a good name because it didn't mean anything.'[6] There is, obviously, an element of facetiousness here. More convincing is Laura Stedman's suggestion that the name 'Luska' was derived from her grandfather's friend and physician, a Dr. Lusk.[7] There may also have been another reason why Harland adopted a pseudonym. In his autobiographical novel, *Grandison Mather*, Harland's hero-writer, Thomas Gardiner, adopts a pen name that is an anagram of his own 'because, if [the book] should be a failure, I don't want to be handicapped by it. I don't want to be saddled with an unsuccessful book. But if it succeeds, I can drop the nom-de-plume, run up my true colors, and no one will be the loser.'[8] However, despite the enormous success of his first novel, Harland continued to use his pseudonym.

Having suggested one or two revisions to Harland, Stedman submitted the manuscript, complete with pseudonym, to O. M. Dunham of Cassell & Co., who wrote on June 3, 1885, that he was prepared to accept it for publication. On the same day, Stedman wrote to Dunham :

I feel sure you will not have cause to regret it. The letter which I received speaks of it as *my manuscript*, but as I fully explained that the author is a young gentleman of 24, I suppose you address me merely as his agent. . . .

And now the best thing I can do is to introduce Mr Luska to you in person, – as he and his publisher ought to have no secrets from one another in this matter. Mr Luska's real name is Harry Harland.[9]

However, a problem arose with respect to Harland's title, for *From Generation to Generation* had already been used for a novel before.[10] Several new titles were rejected by Cassell. Finally, Stedman proposed an acceptable one. In a letter to Harland, who had already discarded several possibilities, including *Mated and Fated*, Stedman wrote on June 12 :

Fate would be better but probably has been used. Besides, the Jews do not believe in *fate*, but in a decree, in 'Thus saith the Lord !' This gives me a new range of ideas. For instance the word 'written' in the sense of predetermined. (Besides your hero's destiny came down in writing.)
> ### As It Was Written:
> #### A Jewish Musician's Story
That I call A-1 – easy to pronounce, original, and shorter than the *Generation* title. The phrase is thoroughly Jewish, and found in the Old Testament as follows: I Kings, XXI, 11 and II Chron. XXX,5.[11]

In early September, with its new title, Harland's first novel appeared. Ernest Neuman, the musician of the title, is the narrator of a strange tale involving the mysterious murder of his fiancée, Veronika, his trial and acquittal, and his years of obscure wandering. With the discovery of his father's portrait and family papers revealing a curse of marital infidelity that has haunted the family, Ernest finds that he must slay his mother's seducer (who turns out to be Veronika's father) in order to lift the curse. Failure to do so would result in his father's spirit taking possession of his body to exact vengeance. The disclosure that Ernest was, in fact,

Veronika's murderer is revealed while he is in a hypnotic trance, an account induced by a strange melody that he has been composing. As the novel ends, he assures the reader that 'the murderer of Veronika Pathzuol meets with the punishment which his crime demands.'

Gothic in its narrative devices (the discovery of the portrait and family papers in a mysterious strongbox, the family curse, the supernatural elements, and the terror of discovering his own guilt) and modern in its depiction of the narrator's *Angst*, Harland's novel is effective popular entertainment, for it is managed with considerable skill. One interesting device, no doubt utilizing Aline's knowledge of music, is the inclusion of a half page of musical notation in order to describe Veronika. As Ernest explains, 'If I wanted to give utterance to my idea of Veronika, all I should have to do would be to take my violin and play this heavenly melody from Chopin's Impromptu in C-sharp minor. . .' Such a device, involving music and its evocative power, suggests Harland's interest in the psychological laws of association, of involuntary memory and the merging of present sensation with past experience, such as we see later in Proust. Not until 1939, in an article by Justin O'Brien, was Harland identified as 'an American forerunner of Proust,' who probably had never read him.[12]

A striking example, cited by O'Brien, of the evocative power of involuntary memory occurs in *As It Was Written*, when Ernest says that he used to cross the Hudson River to New Jersey every week with Veronika and thereby associated his love with ferry-boats : 'The Hoboken ferry-boats became to my thinking vastly more interesting than the most romantic of Venetian gondolas ; and to this day I cannot sniff the peculiar stuffy odor that always pervades a ferry-boat cabin without being transported back across the years to that happy, happy time.'[13] A number of Harland's works contain these moments of lost time recaptured; but Harland, apparently, was unaware that he had discovered an important source of psychological truth. As O'Brien writes: 'Though Henry Harland's total work is less voluminous than Proust's, it contains just as many of these mysterious renewals of the past.' But the major difference between Harland and Proust is that the latter '*consciously* explained and utilized a series of *subconscious* experiences.' That, says O'Brien, is the source of Proust's originality.

Harland's use of the occult has several sources, both personal and fictive. One authority on Harland, Donald A. Roberts, has written that Henry's mother, who was particularly interested in spiritualism, was considered a medium.[14] In addition, at Unitary Home, Charles Wentworth Upham, formerly a pastor of the First Church in Salem, Massachusetts, was at work on a history of witchcraft in that town. Stedman, among others in the settlement, became interested in spiritualism as a result of Upham's research.[15] In the late nineteenth century, the occult had become an increasingly popular subject for fiction; immediately preceding Harland's work on *As It Was Written*, a novel titled *Called Back* (1883) by 'Hugh Conway' (the pseudonym of Frederick J. Fargus) was a sensation: within three years it had sold over 350,000 copies and was translated into several languages and dramatized for the stage. Its author, hitherto an obscure writer, became an instant celebrity. The plot of his novel involves revolutionary intrigue, plots of murder, and a supernatural incident during which the hero, who is blind, visualises a murder. The public response to such unusual material may have prompted Harland to model his first novel after *Called Back*. At the same time, however, he clearly saw the possibility of reaching a specific audience by means of a Jewish setting and characters; such a novel, consisting of supernatural and ethnic elements, would, as Harland wrote to Stedman on April 17, 1885, be 'new.'

The critical reception was impressive. On September 22, 1885, the *New York Daily Tribune's* lead review hailed *As It Was Written* as 'a striking, original and weird tale, full of power and passion and in all respects distinctly out of the common.' The reviewer was especially impressed by the 'working out of so strange and abnormal a plot,' calling it a 'triumph of art' that looks forward to 'further successes.' On October 5, the *New York Times*, noting the influence of *Called Back*, concluded that 'the handiwork is much finer and more artistic than that of the late Mr Fargus.' Remarkable, however, in this review is the first suspicion that Harland was not Jewish : 'It may be shrewdly suspected that Sidney Luska is no Hebrew ; we may go further and decide that he is not a musician in any professional sense. Jews know their race too well ; musicians are too near to their professional brethren to indulge, though it be in romance, in the highly colored flights of this particular Jewish musician. . . .'

The response was far greater than Harland had ever hoped : one review hailed the book as 'one of the most powerful novels of the year' (*St. Louis Republican*) ; another assured readers that it was 'most likely to take a permanent place in literature' (*Yale Courant*). Such excerpts were placed by Cassell's on the back flyleaf of Harland's second novel, *Mrs Peixada*. Some reviewers, however, were less enthusiastic : the reviewer in *The Athenaeum*, on October 10 called the novel 'by far the worst of imitations of *Called Back*,' and in November, the reviewer for the Chicago *Dial* lamented that it was 'undeserving of the name of literature.'

A significant review appeared in the *Jewish Messenger*, a leading English-language periodical in New York devoted to topics of Jewish interest. Generally favourable, the review points to a distinction between George Eliot's *Daniel Deronda* and *As It Was Written: 'In Deronda*, the purpose of the author in plainly told – Judaism is conspicuously presented, and those who have prejudices at the start are not wholly freed from them at the end. This local novel . . . on only one page ascribes direct merit to a people that possess many Veronikas and Neumans and few Pathzuols – its noble purpose of levelling the prejudices between man and man is read between the lines.' Concluding, the reviewer makes a comment that in the light of Harland's subsequent career is rich in irony : '. . . to Sidney Luska we owe a debt of gratitude for charming us with a powerful story, and at the same time contributing more powerfully than could sermons and editorials to the better appreciation of the genius of Judaism.'[16]

The 'one page' ascribing 'direct merit' to the Jews occurs in a speech by Merivale, the only Gentile in the novel, who proclaims that 'the whole future of America depends upon the Jews' :

> It is the Jewish element that is to leaven the whole lump – color the whole mixture. The English element alone is, so to speak, one portion of pure water ; the German element, one portion of *eau sucrée;* now add the Jewish – it is a dose of rich strong wine. It will give fire and flavor to the decoction. The future Americans, thanks to the Jew in them, will have passions, enthusiasms. They will paint great pictures, compose great music, write great poems, be capable of great heroism. . . .'[17]

The *Jewish Messenger*, obviously impressed by Harland's novel, invited him to submit a story to a future issue. In three months, 'A Purim Episode' appeared, occupying three columns on the first page of the 'Double Supplement.'[18] An exercise in pseudo-Gothic horror, the story involves an insane Jewish undertaker's daughter who, sleeeping in a coffin, suddenly rises with a hideous laugh to bite the narrator (who, with two other Jewish boys, had entered the establishment after midnight). Relying on such stylistic clichés as 'hiss of a serpent,' 'the shriek of a ghoul,' and 'blood [that] curdled in our veins,' the story is self-parody, the Jewish element seemingly irrelevant.

At the time of the publication of his first novel, Harland was writing and publishing short stories in various American newspapers (to date, unidentified) that bought them from a syndicate organized in 1884 by Samuel S. McClure, later to achieve fame as publisher of *McClure's Magazine*. Such popular authors as Frank R. Stockton, Julian Hawthorne (son of the famed novelist), and Louise Chandler Moulton wrote for the syndicate, and Harland agreed to do likewise when Stedman introduced him to McClure. In his autobiography, written in collaboration with Willa Cather, one of his authors,[19] McClure recalls that Harland's *As It Was Written* 'was being talked about everywhere' and that Harland had 'a manner at once ingratiating and sincere, and was 'an inveterate smoker of choice cigarettes.'[20]

Harland's generally cordial relationship with McClure encountered difficulty, however, in connection with his second novel, *Mrs Peixada*, scheduled for publication in 1886. Apparently, McClure, in order to enhance Harland's critical reputation and thereby lend greater value to his stories handled by the syndicate, had sent to one of the newspapers some comments attributed to Stedman concerning Harland's forthcoming novel. Irate over the release of these private remarks never intended for publication and over the use of language not actually Stedman's, Harland wrote to McClure on November 25, 1885:

I have just learned that, in communicating with *The Springfield Republican*, you have attributed certain language to Mr E. C. Stedman, respecting *Mrs Peixada*, which that gentleman certainly never could have used, and which I certainly never quoted to you as coming from him. In conversation with you I did say – carelessly – that Mr E. C. Stedman had read my MS. and that he thought thus and so of it. But I did not say that he had expressed himself in any such language as you ascribe to him ; and furthermore I particularly and emphatically cautioned you not merely not to repeat or quote Mr Stedman's private opinion in any form or for any purpose, but also to make no mention of his name in connection with my novel. You have defied my caution and broken confidence with me ; and I therefore make haste to notify you that all relations, either personal or literary, between you and me must forthwith be at an end. Kindly remove my name from your list of authors.[21]

Clearly, Harland was concerned more about his godfather's reputation than about his own future with McClure, for if *Mrs Peixada* were a failure, Stedman would be embarrassed by the high praise attributed to him. On the following day, Harland wrote to Stedman reporting McClure's confession that making use of Stedman's name was 'unpardonable to the last degree' and stating that he professed that 'utmost contrition.' But Harland was uncertain as to McClure's sincerity : 'I have made him promise to write to every newspaper on his list, explaining that he had no authority to mention Mr Stedman, and that, so far as he is aware, Mr Stedman has never expressed any opinion respecting the novel *Mrs Peixada*.' The remainder of the letter reveals Harland's concern for the McClures, with whom he had enjoyed a pleasant relationship :

After [McClure] had made this promise [i.e., to write to every newspaper on his list], came the announcement from me that I meant forthwith to break off all relations with him. He said, 'Well, it will ruin me. It will rob me of the confidence of my newspapers. It will take the bread out of my wife's mouth, and break her heart, besides.' I really feel that I would be justified — and he doesn't dispute it — in absolutely refusing to let him have a line of my writing. But his wife ought to be considered, after all. Poor woman, I don't want to hurt *her*. I don't want to hurt *him*, either.

The letter further describes a visit by the McClures to Beekman Place : Mrs McClure 'had wormed the whole story from him ; and he made my heart ache by the picture he drew of her distress. Well, I told him that I would write to you, and ask your advice. . . I feel that McClure is not a safe man to deal with. . . .'[22]

Harland's laudable preoccupation with his godfather's reputation, his sense that McClure was dishonest and manipulative in his handling of the situation, and his own integrity in the face of possible repercussions from McClure testify to his maturity and honour at the age of twenty-four. Stedman, however, healed the wounds. McClure, after all, could damage any writer's reputation and possibly his livelihood because of his influential position. On December 5, 1885, explaining how McClure had arranged to send out corrections to his previous press release concerning *Mrs Peixada* (though Harland was still not satisfied with them), Harland wrote to Stedman : 'To say "thank you" to you at this junction [*sic*] when you have snatched me from the jaws of literary death – would be to say nothing. I owe you everything – and Aline and I are both conscious of our indebtedness.'[23]

In early 1886, one gathers the extent of Harland's fame and importance from his inclusion in a critical survey titled 'A Half Score New Novelists,' which appeared in the prestigious *Atlantic Monthly*. The reviewer, however, had several reservations about *As It Was Written*, among them the observation that the novel was 'a thin tissue of improbabilities' and that it 'reads to us like a story dashed off at white heat by a writer who was only eager to reach the ingenious device.'[24] Harland, acutely aware of the novel's faults, acknowledged them in a letter to the critic Barrett Wendell : 'You in your letter have simply stated what I have felt all along – you have crystallized what was a vague (but dark) cloud upon my mind. The plot is too far-fetched. Not a doubt about it. I'm never going to do it again. .... I am afraid *that* will kill the book.'[25] Despite these acknowledged faults, sales were phenomenal for a first novel: a reported 50,000 copies ; and, for the most part the reviews, as we have seen, were favourable, at times ecstatic.

In the autumn of 1885, Harland was already at work on *Mrs Peixada*,[26] and with the royalties from *As It Was Written*, he decided in February, 1886, to resign from his clerkship in the Surrogate's office to devote himself entirely to his writing. In March, *The Critic* reported his resignation and, though not the first public disclosure, revealed his true identity.[27] Harland's second novel, *Mrs Peixada*, appeared in April, appropriately dedicated to Daniel G. Rollins, the Surrogate of New York and family friend, for the novel is much concerned with wills. Its central character, Arthur Ripley, a young New York lawyer and the only Gentile in this story, is hired to find Mrs Peixada, who has vanished after her acquittal of the murder of her husband and his coachman on grounds on insanity. A new will has been uncovered that entitles the brother of Mr Peixada to the estate. The central irony occurs when Ripley marries a woman named Mrs Lehmyl, who lives in Beekman Place, and who is, in fact, Mrs Peixada (Harland, however, makes little attempt to prepare the reader for the shock of discovery, for it is obvious who Mrs Lehmyl is early in the novel). Again indicted, she unexpectedly pleads guilty but explains in a letter that she killed in self-defence after learning that her husband and his coachman were thieves planning a murder. On the sole basis of the letter, the charges against her are dropped, and she is freed. Ripley, ailing from the shock, is restored to health by Mrs Peixada, and they leave New York to live in Europe.

The novel is conventionally melodramatic, without the emotional intensity, the psychological probing, or supernaturalism that had made *As It Was Written* interesting entertainment. Like the first novel, *Mrs Peixada* makes use of Jewish characters, expressions, and allusions to Jewish customs as mere local colour. That is, there is little relationship between the plot and its ethnic cast of characters, for in such a story Gentiles would do as well as Jews. Harland includes high praise for Jews again when Ripley remarks : 'On the average, I think the Jews are the kindest-hearted and clearest-minded people one meets here abouts.'[28] But an important note is struck (developed at greater length in his next novel, *The Yoke of the Thorah*, concerning the problem of intermarriage between Gentiles and Jews) when Ripley states : 'I want to see [Jews] intermarry with the Christians – amalgamate, and help form the American people of the future. That of course is their destiny.'[29] But Harland makes no attempt, in *Mrs Peixada*, to present Ripley's marriage to Mrs Peixada as a problem ; like certain laudatory remarks about Jews in *As It Was Written*, Ripley's are entirely gratuitous. Harland had not yet fused his Jewish material to theme and plot within a dramatic framework. The major fault, however, is its contrived happy ending : clearly, Harland had not consulted either his father or Rollins concerning the plausibility of Mrs Peixada's letter being accepted by both the district attorney and the judge.

A review of the novel in the *New York Times* reveals a concern that Harland has not utilized Jewish settings with any accuracy but has exploited them for other ends : 'The story of Jewish life in New York City, the true realistic one, has yet to be written.'[30] Harland's novels, set in the Beekman Place neighbourhood, where there were, apparently, some German Jews living, was in no sense a 'ghetto' (as Ripley calls it in the novel). In 1901, one writer described four 'ghettos' in New York City, two in Manhattan and two in Brooklyn (the 'great Ghetto,' and the most famous, was that on the lower East Side of Manhattan). The Beekman Place neighbourhood is not mentioned.[31]

Most of the other reviews, however, were quite favourable, *The Critic* stating that the novel was 'far above the average murder story in having an undertone of passion very different from the ordinary complications of mere detective difficulties.'[32] But the most enthusiastic review came from the pen of the novelist William Dean Howells, editor of *Harper's New Monthly Magazine*, who regarded 'Sidney Luska' as a disciple of his own creed of realism 'because in this second venture of his he has left the region of music and romance where he dwelt in his first story, and has stepped quite out into the light of our common day. . . .'[33] Praising the depiction of Jews in the novel (and clearly disagreeing with the review in the *New York Times*), Howells writes of 'Mr Luska's mastery in the treatment of his various Israelites, in their presentation individually, and in their collective localization here in New York. They are neither flattered nor caricatured ; they are simply portrayed with truth by a hand that is already firm and that gives promise of greater and greater skill.'

Harland, pleased with the review, voiced the belief, in a letter to Stedman, that his godfather was at least partly responsible for the high praise. On a trip in Europe with Aline (having left New York on May 8),[34] Harland wrote from Paris :

> You will imagine the surprise and delight and encouragement with which I have read what Mr Howells has to say of *Mrs Peixada* in this month's *Harper's*. But my reason for writing to you is that I wish to give voice to a suspicion which has taken root and ripened in Aline's breast and in my own. The effect of that suspicion is that *you are somehow at the bottom of it*, as you are at the bottom of most of the good things which happen to us. . . .'[35]

Three days later, Harland received a letter from Stedman informing him that the *Atlantic Monthly* was interested in publishing as a serial *Elias Bacharach*, his third novel, whose title was later changed to the more provocative *The Yoke of the Thorah*.[36] It was, as Harland pointed out in a letter to Stedman, a 'curious coincidence' that one year ago on June 5, his godfather had informed him that his first novel had been accepted. At work on his third novel, Harland describes his and Aline's Parisian life:

> We are established in a sunny little room over here on the South side of the Seine, near to the Luxembourg Gardens, and among the students. Our life is a very regular one. We don't go sight-seeing. We work – Aline at her music and I at my writing. In the evening we go to the theater, or sit out at a Café table upon the Boulevard ; and that is the full extent of our dissipation. We have numberless French friends, and a few Americans, and so we are never lonesome. We drink daily out of your silver cup, smoke from your cigarette case, and make notes in your little blank book. But we need no such material tokens to make us think of you. We are indebted to you for all our good fortune – for the fact, among others, that we are here in Paris now.[37]

The Harlands remained in Paris until mid-September, when they returned to New York. Before departing, Harland wrote to Stedman that *Elias Bacharach* was 'nearly finished,' expecting to complete it by November 1st. His evaluation of the manuscript and his comparison with his previous novels are of particular interest:

> Of course, it is very far from perfect ; but it is as good as I, with my present abilities, can make it. I have worked at it in a 'sad sincerity.' I have tried honestly throughout to make it true and genuine. The plot is interesting and *human*, not artificial as the plot of *Mrs Peixada* was, nor mystical as the plot of *As It Was Written* was. The climax is dramatic and terrible, but not at all blood-and-thunderish. I think there is a good deal of real, deep emotion here and there. And everywhere, I believe, it

is refined. I feel sure that it will give my reputation a decided lift.[38]

Harland was looking forward to its serialization (he alludes to this several times in his letters to Stedman), hoping that the *Atlantic Monthly* would take it since they had shown interest in it, but Thomas Bailey Aldrich, the magazine's editor and Stedman's friend, seems to have changed his mind. In a letter to Stedman in July, Harland revealed his disappointment in Aldrich's silence: 'Unless I succeed in placing *Elias* as a serial, it will be bad for my reputation and bad for my purse.'[39] He found such major periodicals as *Harper's*, *Scribner's*, and *The Century Magazine* closed to him, possibly because he wished to have his novel accepted for serialization before completion and, upon completion, expected immediate publication. (One periodical editor informed him that only when it was completed would he consider it for serialization, which could not occur sooner than one year after acceptance.)[40] Earlier, Harland had lamented to Stedman: '. . . it is a fact that none of the younger American novelists has had better reviews or better sales than I have had. I confess to a certain feeling of discouragement. It's a serious thing to begin a novel that will take 18 months or two years to write, without any prospects of being able profitably to place it when it is finished.'[41]

Disappointed with his failure to serialize his third novel, Harland again signed a contract with Cassell & Co., the publisher of almost all of his 'Sidney Luska' novels. *The Yoke of the Thorah*, appearing in May of 1887, is the best of his early novels, despite structural weaknesses, for Harland had finally utilised a Jewish setting in the service of character and theme. The major conflict of its central character, Elias Bacharach, in his wish to marry a Christian, grows out of an orthodox horror of intermarriage. Elias' uncle, a rabbi, interprets the love of a Christian as 'a spiritual disease' and intermarriage as the 'most deadly [sin] of all.' For Elias, however, the conflict cannot be resolved, for his love of Christine (the name obviously symbolic) transcends religious restrictions.

During the marriage ceremony, Elias suddenly has an epileptic seizure and collapses. His uncle, who had foreseen that God would never permit such a marriage to occur, tells Elias, now convinced that God indeed had interceded, that his fiancé is 'a Christian, a Goy, despised and abominated of the Lord. She has served her purpose [i.e., to bring Elias back to the fold of orthodox Judaism]. Now she must bear her punishment.'[42] Christine's father, on discovering from Elias that the marriage is off, explodes angrily : '. . . if it does kill her, I-I'd rather have *it*, by God ! than have her married to you, now that I know what you are, you damn, miserable, white-livered Jew !'[43]

This scene occurs less than half way through the novel ; what follows is a prolonged, at times tiresome, account of Elias' involvement with a Jewish family and his subsequent marriage to a rather uncultured Jewish girl, with whom he has an indifferent life. At the end of the novel, however, Elias by chance sees Christine leaving a concert hall ; he is again passionately inflamed by her vision and, discovering that she is to be married, writes a lengthy, emotional letter begging her to see him at their favourite meeting place in Central Park. But it is not to take place, for Elias, alone and rejected, dies of another epileptic seizure, a scene quite pathetic, without the searing elevation of tragedy, suggesting that the theme was beyond Harland's powers. He permits the device of the epileptic seizure to determine the outcome of the plot, a physiological event that has little relevance to the possibilities of human failure.

Harland handles the story with considerable ambiguity and ambivalence, which resulted in a number of accusations of anti-Semitism in his depiction of Jewish narrow-minded-ness. The *Jewish Messenger*, in which Harland had previously published a story, printed an excerpt from the novel, significantly the scene concerned with Elias' conflicts over his forthcoming marriage to Christine. In editorial remarks, the periodical points out that disapproval of intermarriage was based not on the presumed superiority of Jews but on the likelihood of marital discord from religious differences.[44] A fortnight later, an 'Open Letter : To the Author of *The Yoke of the Thorah*,' signed by 'Cyril,' appeared in the *Messenger*, substantially stating the same position as that of the editorial – namely, that the novel was an 'anachronism' : '. . . in New York City, such Jews [as Elias and his uncle] never were and are never likely to be – Jews who speak so classic an English and who are influenced by such medievalism and superstition.' On the more serious question of anti-Christian attitudes among Jews, the 'Open-Letter' continues : '. . . most readers will say : "There, didn't I tell you how narrow the Jews are, how they hate us Christians, how they regard themselves as a superior race and will not intermarry, from a holy terror of Christian contamination?" I would not imply that your idea was to teach such prejudice ; but the story teaches it.'[45]

Despite the fact that *The Yoke of the Thorah* had appeared in the spring, attacks by some of Harland's Jewish critics were still continuing by the autumn. The *Messenger*, on October 28, reported that 'Mr Harlan' (so spelled throughout) was being abused ; however, the newspaper defended him as 'a gentleman singularly free from prejudice' without any of the 'malice of an anti-Semitic scribe.' Grateful to the *Messenger* for its defence of his character, Harland wrote to the editor in a letter dated October 31, 1887 :

> I beg you to accept my sincere thanks for the kind things the *Messenger* has been saying in my behalf. I am glad to learn that you personally do not share the mis-

understanding of the spirit of my books which prevails generally among the Jewish reading public; and in bringing the *Messenger's* influence to bear toward clearing that misunderstanding up, you have rendered me a service the value of which I could scarcely overestimate.[46]

Apart from Harland's difficulty with some Jewish critics, the general reception of his novel was quite mixed, many of the reviews pointing to the power of the writing in many scenes but also to the weakness of the central design. Clearly, Harland had strengthened his reputation, for despite the critical reservations, he had written a controversial novel that was being widely discussed. Harland was concerned, however, about Howells' reaction. A lengthy letter to Howells, written on September 3, is filled with doubts, not only about *The Yoke of the Thorah* but also about his own ability to be 'true' to life and about Jews as subject matter. One of Harland's most important unpublished revelations, it deserves extended quotation:

As for *The Yoke of the Thorah*, I am sure you won't like it. Looking it over now, I can see that it is strained and romantic, and that the deus-ex-machina is its chief actor; yet while I was writing it I really fancied that it was realistic and true to life. Isn't it a significant circumstance, that a fellow can write a thing with the desire to do true work, and with the belief that he *is* doing true work, and yet as a matter of fact be floundering around a thousand miles away from the plane of actual life? It illustrates the great difficulty of being true, of distinguishing the true from the false; that eternal vigilance is the price of truth. When I am writing I keep asking, 'Is this true? Is this the way it would happen in real life?' But I find it very hard to decide yes or no; and then, as soon as I have decided, I feel distrustful of the correctness of my decision. I should suppose that this must be the experience of every young man who possesses no magic touchstone, and is not a heaven-born 'genius.'

—As for the Jewry, all my friends are urging me to abandon it. I am going to use it a little in a young folk's serial that I am now writing for *Wide Awake;*[47] but after that I think I shall leave it for a while, to turn to some other phases of New York life which seem to me of great interest and importance. But the Jewry is an immense and fruitful field of which I have only most inadequately touched the outside edge. This numerous, gifted, ambitious race, so recently relieved of its disabilities, its own life, and the interaction of its life with that of the community round about it, must be of enduring interest. But the Jews don't want to be written about; at least, they don't want to be portrayed as they really are. Your picture must flatter them; otherwise they'll feel like crucifying you. But in this respect they don't differ much from other people, I suppose.[48]

Earlier, Harland had written to Howells thanking him for his approval of a short story, 'A Land of Love,' which had appeared in *Lippincott's Monthly Magazine* in August. Harland's friends, critical of the story, had called it 'stale, flat, unprofitable,' and even the editors of *Lippincott's,* Harland informed Howells, had objected that the story wasn't 'sensational' enough. Harland continues: 'While I was writing the story, Mrs Harland and I kept wondering, "How will Mr Howells like it? Will it strike him as a step in the right direction?" ' In this lengthy letter, Harland writes as though he were participating in a ritual of conversion to the doctrine of realism in order to please his mentor:

. . . although my first two stories were romantic and melodramatic, – because I had no definite notion of the proper function of fiction, and because it is *easier* to handle the materials of romance than to handle truths, – I should like you to know that the conviction has steadily been growing in me that the highest work the novelist can do is to deal with the realities of human life and nature. And that I may some time perhaps be able to write a novel in which the deus-ex-machina shall have

33

no part whatever, but which shall truthfully illustrate actual human experiences, and be in the best sense realistic, is the ambition which guides my labors. I can't help believing – it seems to me self-evident, indisputable, in spite of the fact that it is disputed at every turn – that if anything in this world is worth doing, telling the truth about men and women is. It seems to me that that truth must be far more interesting than any romance, that it needs no romantic coloring or accessories to make it interesting ; that, of all interesting things, it must be the one which is of most supreme and vital interest.[49]

Clearly, Harland's desire to write a 'truly realistic novel' – from a belief, shared with Howells, that realism is closest to 'nature' and 'human life' – reveals a confusion in his thinking that 'truth' and 'realism' are synonymous, for, in point of fact, realism is only one of several modes of expression for revealing 'truth' – 'romance' being another. Throughout his early career, Harland moved uncertainly between realism and romance, though obviously attracted to the darker, more sensational side of life.

In the most recent critical attention to Harland, David Cheshire and Malcolm Bradbury have written that, whereas at the end of the nineteenth century American fiction became increasingly realistic, there was a counter-movement among some writers, Harland among them, who sought an escape from realism's preoccupation with the strictness of cause and effect, verisimilitude, psychological development of character, and social consciousness. Such a reaction to realism, Cheshire and Bradbury contend, was the result of extensive American travel in Europe, which became the characteristic setting for the 'romance.' The tendency, as we see it progressively in Harland, was toward melodrama and idyll – indeed, in the later Anglo-Italian novels, with their depiction of pastoral settings free of the disturbing elements of evil, idyll becomes form and style.[50] Early in his career, however, Harland had not resolved, as Henry James had, the apparent contradiction between realism and romance. The two major influences at the outset of Harland's career, Stedman and Howells, continued to pull in opposite directions, a situation that did not particularly work to Harland's benefit.

By early 1888, an indication of Harland's fame may be gauged by *The Critic's* invitation to participate in a survey of well-known American writers on whether they believed it was necessary – as Horace had implied – for an author to 'suffer' with his own characters – a naive question, to be sure, but one calculated to interest the general reader. Twenty-three responses appeared in the March 24th issue (Mark Twain answered with one word: 'Yes'). Harland, identified as 'H. Harland (Sidney Luska),' responded in a paragraph, dated March 4, 1888, concisely delineating the divided nature of the artist and the proper aesthetic distance that is essential in the act of creation :

> I must put myself in my character's place, and experience his emotions, joyful and sorrowful, or else I can't write about him at all; yet at the same time, I must retain my own identity sufficiently to analyze and understand his emotions, or else I can't write about him intelligibly. So, practically, I have to chop myself into two men, one of whom suffers and enjoys in dead earnest, while the other in cold blood examines him, feels his pulse, and notes his symptoms. If the latter individual for a moment loses his equipoise, my work becomes hysterical and incoherent; while if the former forgets his passion, and becomes indifferent, the work will be cold, hard, and artificial. To judge from my own experience, therefore, Horace told just one half of the truth.

At this time, an odd incident occurred involving Aline, of whom a rumour was circulating that she was Jewish. And, oddly enough, the rumour was attributed to E. C. Stedman. Harland, however, in a letter to Charles H. Webb, editor of the New York *World*, assured him that Stedman 'emphatically denies' having told anyone that Aline was a Jewess. 'On the contrary,' Harland wrote, 'whenever [Stedman] has had occasion to say who she is, he has said, "She's a niece of Professor Merriam of Columbia." ' [51] In the margin of her husband's letter, Aline wrote : 'Dear Mr Webb, Isn't it funny to think of Harry's being caught in his own trap ? You can have no idea how grieved he is to think I have been reputed a Jewess – 6 shades of Mrs Peixada and Veronika ! ! ! As for me I take it to heart only because I am so proud of being a Frenchwoman and the granddaughter of my grandfather. A.M.H.' Harland's reaction to the rumour, one would imagine, might have been that of quiet amusement (as Aline was amused, though simultaneously offended). It reveals, however, a curious ambivalence, particularly if one recalls his urging, in *The Yoke of the Thorah*, of intermarriage between Gentile and Jew, for though he proposes it in the world of the novel, he was outraged and grieved over the mere rumour that *he* was married to a Jewess, as though he had been touched by some form of contamination.

Harland's next novel, *My Uncle Florimond*, on which he had been working through much of 1887, appeared in late 1888. A new departure for Harland, it is concerned with a boy's loss of innocence concerning his uncle (in one sense, a symbolic reflection, on a different level, of the situation in *The Yoke of the Thorah*). Its cover, depicting a boy standing on a pier with a bag in his hands, gazing at a passing ship, reveals its central intent : Harland's wish to write an adventure novel for young readers. Jewish characters in New York play a major role in the life of the young boy, who travels from Norwich in search of his Uncle Florimond. For the first time, the title page, citing 'Sidney Luska' as the author, includes Harland's name in parentheses beneath the pseudonym. The novel was widely regarded as a minor work, and Howells, who received an inscribed copy from Harland, did not review it in *Harper's*.

In November of 1888, Mrs Howells sent Harland a copy of George Moore's *Confessions of a Young Man*, which had recently appeared. Harland's letter to her contains an interesting critical judgment of Moore and, what is more, an attack on Moore's shallow version of French Decadence:

> In parts I found it rather amusing, though the author's constant straining after originality and his consuming desire to reveal his familiarity with recondite French literature were rather tiresome. As for his measure of Mr Howells, was it not simply silly and puerile?[52] I don't believe he has read Mr Howells at all. His sort of cynicism and originality is after all very cheap and shallow, and I should think it would be very easy. Let us decry all that is sweet, natural, wholesome, and go in for all that is malarial, artificial, extravagant. For a pet we will keep a Python. We will love all that the world hates, even if it is bad and deserves hatred. We will hate all that the world loves, even if it is good and deserves to be loved. A sort of conventionalized unconventionality, cut-and-dried, made by rule.[53]

In view of Harland's later career as dandy and poseur, his condemnation of Moore in 1888 is ironic, and though he thought that Moore's 'consuming desire to reveal his familiarity with recondite French literature' was tiresome, Harland himself was later to cavort with Decadents and Symbolists in Paris.

In the late 1880s, Harland's energies seemed limitless: novels and stories followed one another with astonishing speed. In January, 1889, he had already completed a play, which he offered to the theatrical impresario, Augustin Daly: 'I have written a short farce, with four characters, entitled *The Tale of an Overcoat*, cast in New York, at the present time. . . . This is my first essay in the line of dramatic composition.'[54] This play, apparently unproduced, has never been published (and the manuscript's whereabouts are unknown). Early in 1889, two additional volumes appeared with Sidney Luska's name on the title page and with Harland's in parentheses beneath. *Grandison Mather*, previously mentioned, is an autobiographical novel; and *A Latin-Quarter Courtship and Other Stories* contains four stories, the longest being 'A Latin-Quarter Courtship,' which had appeared in *Lippincott's* (August, 1887) under the title 'A Land of Love.'

As 'A Latin-Quarter Courtship' suggests, the setting is Paris and its characters are French and American Bohemians, not Jews. (This was not the first time that Harland had not written of Jews: a tale of little significance, 'The Story of Angela,' with an Italian-American setting, had appeared in *Lippincott's* in January, 1887.) The Parisian setting was no doubt suggested by the Harlands' stay on the Left Bank in 1886; possibly, Harland's earlier visit to Europe in 1883 also contributed to it. The romantic intrigue of the American novelist Stephen Ormizon with the attractive Denise Personnette, half-French and half-American (no doubt modelled after Aline), provides the central motive, and the gaiety of *la vie de Bohème* provides local colour. In the same volume, Harland included 'Mr Sonnenschein's Inheritance,' a story rich in Jewish folk humour that tells the ironic tale of the loss and recovery of money deposited by Mr Sonnenschein in a friend's safe. In this volume, the two masks of Henry Harland come together for the first time: two worlds, mutually antagonistic (as Albert Parry has written, Bohemians were distrustful of Jews, whom they identified with the commercial Philistine world rather than the irresponsible world of the artist)[55] yet seemingly two sides of the same coin, for both groups – Jews and Bohemians – were outcasts living in their self-enclosed worlds.

Grandison Mather, which appeared a few weeks after

A Latin-Quarter Courtship and Other Stories, is again concerned with an artist, this time a novelist, and his attempt to achieve fame. The novel has obvious autobiographical elements: Tom Gardiner uses the pseudonym of 'Grandison Mather'; he is helped by an older writer, a prominent member of the literary establishment, modelled after Stedman; Tom's wife, Rose, is a singer who completes her husband's second novel (an odd prophecy, for though Aline never did this during her husband's lifetime, she did complete his final novel, left unfinished at his death). When Tom and Rose, because of monetary troubles, move from their elegant apartment, they settle in 53 Beekman Place; and their landlord is a Mr Grickel, a German Jew, who leads a congregation of liberal Jews called the Society for Humane Culture, clearly Harland's depiction of Felix Adler and the Ethical Culture Society. At the end of the novel, Tom is elected to the Authors Club, as indeed Harland was. The novel concludes on a sentimental note about the joys of marriage.

Before its publication, Harland wrote to Stedman that the novel would be the 'flattest of failures.'[56] The critical reception, however, was quite favourable. *The Critic* rhapsodized: 'Not a dull line, not a careless sentence, not an improbable situation or an untrue picture is there from cover to cover.'[57] The most important review – and most appreciated by Harland – appeared in *Harper's*, written by Howells, who also included a consideration of *A Latin-Quarter Courtship and Other Stories*. Harland, Howells wrote, 'makes in these later books a frank advance on the realistic lines while keeping enough of the romantic thaumaturgy to please the reader of his earlier fiction.' Howells concludes by declaring Harland a 'Grade A realist' in his 'sense of his responsibility to something better than your curiosity, and nothing that is good is sacrificed to any mere literary end in his work. The praise seems negative, but it has its positive side, too; for the finest work of our day teaches that to be morally false is to be aesthetically false.'[58]

Stedman was distressed by Howell's review, for he believed that realism was not Harland's happiest medium. In later years, Howells recalled the disagreement with Stedman in a letter to Laura Stedman:

> I remember once he gave me quite a scolding because he thought I had put Harry Harland on the wrong track. . . . I noticed two or three of the books ; as I was an intense realist, I praised what seemed a tendency to realism in them. After that Harland wrote a realistic novel. It was an account of art student life in Paris. It was very well done, but your grandfather thought it was a false step and that it was out of the line of Harland's natural genius . . . he didn't think it was the thing for Harry Harland, who was naturally and incurably romantic.[59]

In his desire to lure Harland away from Howells' influence, Stedman may have enlisted the support of his friend William Sharp, who wrote under the pseudonym of the romantic Celt 'Fiona Macleod,' for his review in *The Academy*, six months after Howells', reads like a direct reply. At the outset, Sharp states that the author of *Grandison Mather* is 'certainly in the front rank of the younger American novelists' and that his latest novel is his most impressive achievement. However, Sharp warns Harland against continuing in the realistic mode, the 'method, broadly speaking, of Mr W. D. Howells':

> It is a method that is excellent for certain episodical themes, but one that seems to me apt to be fatal for creative production of a more ample nature. In dealing so minutely with subservient details the novelist is tempted unconsciously to dwell with equal exactitude upon the irrelevant as upon the most essential. . . . So bright and well-equipped a novelist as Mr Harland

should, above all things, bear in mind that useful and artistic as photography is, it is not, nor ever can be, absolute art.[60]

Despite Harland's admiration for Howells and his appreciation of Howells' reviews of his books, the doctrine and method of realism seemed to have little effect upon Harland, who, as Howells himself admitted, was 'incurably romantic.' In May, 1889, Harland wrote to J. M. Stoddart, editor of *Lippincott's*, that he was at work on a novelette, some 30,000 words in length, 'which has recently run through a newspaper syndicate under the title *Metamorphosis*, and which I am now re-writing under a new title, namely *The Strange Story of Two Women*. It is by all means the most interesting, the most exciting, perhaps (if you love the word) the most *sensational* story I have written.'[61] There would be, however, a delay in its completion, for the Harlands suddenly decided to spend at least a year in England. Writing to Stedman in July, Harland revealed their intentions :

Very suddenly Aline and I have made up our minds to sail with my mother and father for England on the 24th of this month ; and we two younger Harlands at present intend to settle down in or near London, and to remain there for a year or longer. Of course we may be unable to bear the lonesomeness, and so come back sooner ; but at present it looks very like a year. I promise you, our hearts are heavy at the prospect ; but it seems to us expedient and wise.[62]

The letter does not suggest the American *émigré's* rejection of his homeland ; indeed, the Harlands concern over 'lonesomeness' reveals a decided uncertainty as to their choice. They had, after all, many friends in New York, and they had never lived in London. Why they chose London is unknown ; it had, as Harland wrote to Mr & Mrs Howells, the 'attraction and novelty' that they looked forward to, but, he added, 'on the whole we are feeling pretty blue and homesick –

especially when we realize how long a separation it threatens between us and the friends we love here.'[63]

But the vibrant, witty Harland and his talented wife, fortified by letters of introduction from Stedman, who entertained them on 'their farewell call' on July 17,[64] soon found themselves among the great and the near-great of London literary circles. Indeed, the vitality of the 1890s in the British capital took such a hold upon Harland that he did not return to America until 1902.

CHAPTER THREE

An American in London (1889-1894)

B EFORE SETTLING IN London, the Harlands spent some time in Wales and Paris. On August 16, Harland wrote to Stedman from Wales that he was 'doing no work' : 'I don't like the idleness ; and we shall be glad when we get settled down somewhere, and I can renew my liaison with my pen.'[1] By November, they were back in London, living at Alfred Place West, Thurlow Square. In a lengthy and lively letter to the Stedmans, Aline wrote 'from the darkness of this sunless and misty city' to tell them of their adventures :

> If I had realized what a place London is in Winter I am afraid Harry, with all his powers of persua- sion, would not have dragged me from Paris the bright, Paris the beautiful, Paris where the sun shines even while the Heavens pour. But now we are settled in lodgings for the Winter, in South Kensington, near friends, and our time is beginning to be so much taken up by dinner parties and five o'clock teas that there is not much left for refusing. People are charming to us, and it is all owing to you, as usual. . . . Your letter to Andrew Lang, the first one we presented, has been more than honoured. Immediately upon receipt of it, Harry was invited to dine with him at the Oxford and Cam- bridge Club, where he was presented to George Saints- bury, Pollock, Rider Haggard, Longman, of Longman and Green & several others, editors and reviewers chiefly . . . they greeted him and treated him with great

cordiality. The next thing Mr Lang did was to put him up the following day at the Savile Club of which all the literary men of note in London are members, for a year. . . . Of course the Savile Club is invaluable and pleasant to Harry. He meets all those men who generally lunch there – and he dines with Walter Besant there this evening. He has quite lost his heart to Besant, who is a lovely, unaffected and enthusiastic man. . . . We have enquired about Gosse here. He hasn't a friend. Everyone says he is envious, spiteful, and exceedingly 'mauvaise langue.'[2]

Aline's letter tells of their meeting with William Sharp, who was to publish his laudable review of Harland in *The Academy*, and urges Stedman to come to London : 'We could all go to Hampstead where the Sharps are, and make a little colony of transplanted Americans and for the space of the season illuminate London with wit & brilliancy enough to last it for the coming Winter.' An interesting comment passes almost parenthetically on the English : '. . . in the main I find Englishmen and Englishwomen so lacking in specific levity as to be almost oppressive.' Harry, she writes, is 'always hard at work, he of course allows nothing to interfere with his morning and finds he can work better & for a longer stretch at a time than at home, where he used to get frightfully nervous.' This last remark may be a clue to the Harlands' sudden departure from New York.

Their life in London is again described in a letter to Howells from Harland, who wrote on December 30 :

We are leading a quiet, regular, and on the whole very pleasant existence in this howling wilderness of fog – (for three days we've not been able to see without lamplight) – but occasionally we get very homesick. . . . I am shortly to bring out here and in America a 'shilling shocker,' which I warn you not to read, as it is very very bad. After that – a semi-theological, semi-metaphysical, little booklet, which is better, but I dare say very bad.'[3]

In one sense, this was Harland's way of informing Howells that for an 'incurable romantic' the method of realism was uncongenial. Harland's mercurial mind needed the stimulation of a variety of modes, preferably the sensational.

Early in 1890, Cassell & Co. published the two short books mentioned in Harland's letter, one of which he had been working on before he left America. The two volumes reveal new departures for Harland, though not happy ones, for they are less fictional narratives than philosophical speculations on free will and determinism, occasioned, no doubt, by the widespread debate generated by Darwin's *Origin of Species* since its publication in 1859.

The first of these two volumes, *Two Voices*, contains two lengthy stories, one of which, 'Dies Irae,' reveals the obvious influence of Zolaesque naturalism. The central character, who kills himself in his determination to embrace hell as his destiny, states: 'What I do is the unavoidable result of who I am . . . the unavoidable result of my heredity and my environment.' In the other story, 'De Profundis,' the speaker, a 'naturalist' in his denial of free will, also proclaims that he is the product of his heredity and environment; thus, necessity compels his actions, in this case the mistreatment of his wife.

The same preoccupation with philosophical questions informs *Two Women or One?*, which appeared shortly after *Two Voices*. However, as Harland described the work to Howells, it is compelling entertainment as a 'shilling shocker.' The story involves a physician who, having saved a young woman from suicide, discovers that she is an escaped convict (she describes herself as 'totally depraved'). He proposes to operate on her skull to obliterate all remembrance of an evil past. After the operation succeeds, she eventually marries a young sculptor (who had known her before but cannot recognise her). On their European honeymoon, she suddenly goes blind. She undergoes an operation to restore her sight, but the effect is also to reverse the condition of her obliterated memory of the past. She now recalls that her husband was one she had formerly hated; overcome by shock, she falls into unconsciousness and dies. The two personalities of the young woman recall Stevenson's *Dr Jekyll and Mr Hyde* (1886), but perhaps the most immediate influence is Edward Bellamy's *Dr Heidenhoff's Process* (1880), in which the hero dreams that his beloved loses her memory of an evil past through an electric shock. Indeed, Bellamy's novel is mentioned during a discussion of the young woman's operation in *Two Women or One?*.

For the first time, the two volumes appeared under Harland's own name, but his pseudonym was placed in parentheses below. One wonders whether Harland objected to the continued existence of 'Sidney Luska' or whether the publisher, wishing to capitalize on the name, insisted on adding it on the title page. There is ample evidence that Harland wished to forget his earlier novels after he had taken up residence in London, as though the mask of 'Sidney Luska' were now a hindrance. When Samuel McClure, on a visit to London, 'threatened' to republish all of the 'Sidney Luska' novels, Harland responded: 'If you do, Sam, I'll publish a statement that Sam McClure is the author of every one of them!'[4] Arthur Waugh, who knew Harland well, has written that Harland was 'ashamed' of his early novels and that he was anxious 'to live their reputation down'[5] and, according to Aline, Harland called his early novels *'mes péchés de jeunesse.'*[6] Indeed, as late as 1901, in a letter to the publisher T. Fisher Unwin, Harland was still unwilling to allow republication of his early novels. He alludes to his former mask as though it were entirely divorced from himself: '. . . as for those early novels attributed to me, I almost think they were written by another man. At any rate, they are very crude and immature performances ; and nothing on earth could induce me to consent to their re-appearance.'[7]

In July, 1890, Harland published a translation of *Fantasia*, an Italian novel by Matilde Serao[8], for Heinemann's International Library, whose general editor was Gosse. Since Harland had had no previous experience as a translator and since his Italian, one may presume, was not really adequate to the task, Gosse asked Paul Sylvester to act as co-translator. Curiously, the American edition, published by the John W. Lovell Co., under the series title 'Lovell's Series of Foreign Literature,' did not include Sylvester's name as co-translator. Presumably, the publisher wished to seize upon Harland's name : the title page gives the 'Luska' pseudonym in parentheses, spelling the first name 'Sydney,' which has been a source of confusion and error ever since.

When Harland arrived in London, he no doubt had a letter of introduction to Gosse from Stedman, close friends for many years. Gosse and Harland found each other congenial company (despite the former's 'mauvaise langue') ; indeed, Gosse became Harland's mentor just as Stedman had been in America, and Harland often addressed Gosse in letters as 'Dear Master.' Waugh has written that Harland became 'one of the most regular of the Gosses's Sunday guests.'[9] On one occasion, Harland 'started a competition [with Gosse] to outdo one another in examples of the banality of popular American literature. Harland's trump card was a story of passion and parted love, when the heroine bowed herself in tears before the man of her affections, and "pressed her brow against his knee with such feverish violence that the pattern of his pants was printed between her eyes in brilliant scarlet." '[10]

By the end of 1890, the Harlands were established in their flat at 144 Cromwell Road, which was to become one of the symbolic centres of the literary world of the 1890s. They kept Stedman informed of their social life, and in a lengthy letter to his godfather, Harland wrote that they hoped to visit New York in April and remain for the summer (a journey that did not materialize). More serious, though, is his remark concerning his lack of strength and an allusion to prior lung trouble : 'Ever since I had my bleeding of the lungs [in 1889], I have been rather unwell. It has cost me every pennyweight of my strength to do my daily stint of fiction. When that was finished I have found myself all used up, a limp rag, with no power of writing in me.' However, a major portion of this important and interesting letter consists of his impressions of new friends :

> Whistler is the best friend we have made here : a most eccentric, kind-hearted, brilliant, delightful creature. He is not so brilliant as E. C. S[tedman], nor so kind-hearted : but he comes second after him among the people whom we know. That these two men should meet and know and like each other is an earnest desire of Aline's and mine. After Whistler I think the man we like best in London is Edmund Gosse. We were horribly afraid of him in the beginning of our acquaintance, for he has a reputation for a *mauvaise langue :* but to us he has been all kindness. Walter Besant we like too, and Henry James. Lang is London's Gilder :[11] he has the big head to an alarming degree. Rudyard Kipling is amusing, Haggard is an overgrown schoolboy. Thomas Hardy, who lives at Dorchester, but comes to town a good deal, is also interesting, but not up to his books. William Sharp has gone to pass the winter in Italy. . . .
>
> We are now domiciled in a flat of our own in South Kensington, and no longer at the tender mercies of the keepers of lodging houses. Our pictures, our books, and the best part of our furniture, we had sent to us, so that, in our drawing-room, your portrait smiles at us from the top of the music-case you gave Aline. We had of course to buy a lot of furniture also, and it was great fun going about the old curiosity shops

of London and picking up Chippendale for a song.[12]

Despite his health, Harland completed another novel by the end of 1890, which he tentatively titled *Fools' Fire* but which was published in the following spring as *Mea Culpa*, the lengthiest of his works. The story, concerned with political refugees from Russia living in Paris, is a decided falling off from his earlier works in its structural weakness and wooden characters. Wrote *The Athenaeum:* 'Three prettily covered volumes are eked out with an amount of vain repetition on the part of the soliloquizing heroine such as is seldom, if ever, met with even in a moral tale.'[13] Gosse read the novel and wrote to give his critical judgment directly to Harland, who appreciated Gosse's 'pointing out the bad' as well as the good in his 'poor three-volume novel.' Harland agreed with Gosse 'that the story does degenerate into melodrama: and of all literary pinchbeck, melodrama is the variety which I personally detest the most. Of course I didn't realise that my puppets were becoming melodramatic while I was "whittling" at them; but I realise it all too clearly now.'[14]

In the spring of 1892, a consultation with doctors about Harland's lung condition resulted in a bad prognosis. Aline wrote to Mrs Stedman several months later that it fell like a 'thunderbolt' upon them and had been a source of anxiety and fear: 'It sometimes seems to me that I have lost my buoyancy and lightheartedness forever. The shock was even more for Harry — yet we have refused to believe all the doctors said, and every sign of improvement gives us courage. . . . Every now and then he is able to work but he is not able to work steadily as he used [to].'[15] In September, the Harlands, in company with Daniel G. Rollins, his brother, and Harland's mother, travelled to Germany and France. Wrote Aline: 'The trip has done Harry a world of good — he enjoyed it and found his lost appetite, and an impetus to get to work again.'[16]

In November, Harland wrote to Stedman about his illness, which seriously affected his work ('I have written nothing but a handful of short stories. . . .'), but in his letter, Harland reveals a new attitude toward the novel: 'I am coming to lose my faith in the *novel* as a form of fiction, and I think of the short-story more and more as the thing desirable.'[17] His changing attitude toward the longer form of fiction may have been prompted by his failing strength, the result of what was diagnosed as tuberculosis. However, he was attracted, as were many others at the end of the nineteenth century, to the short story as an aesthetically promising *genre*, and his later editorship of *The Yellow Book* provided him not only with further stimulus but also with an immediate source of publication.

Having recovered some of his strength, Harland left London with Aline for Paris early in March of 1893, where he worked on short stories for the new periodical *Black and White*.[18] In April, Gosse joined them, and at his request, Harland led him on a tour of the Symbolist haunts along the Boulevard Saint-Michel: 'I determined to haunt that neighborhood with a butterfly-net,' Gosse later wrote, 'and see what delicate creatures with powdery wings I could catch.'[19] Relying on Harland, 'who knows his Paris like the palm of his hand' and who, 'with enthusiastic kindness,' offered to be his cicerone, Gosse set off on his adventure. Harland, however, did not particularly share Gosse's interest in the 'Symbolo-decadent movement, and the ideas of the "poètes abscons comme la lune" left him a little cold, yet he entered at once into the sport of the idea.' For three days, Gosse and Harland successfully captured Symbolist and Decadent butterflies in their natural habitats, including 'that really substantial moth, Verlaine.' The adventure included the quaffing of 'a number of highly indigestible drinks' and listening to recitations of obscure poems; the lively climax came with dinner in the company of various poets, including Verlaine, at the Restaurant d'Harcourt. 'The expedition,' wrote Gosse, 'was a great success.'

After Gosse departed, Harland wrote to him to sympathize with his attack of rheumatism : '. . . we devoutly hope it is in no wise a consequence of our goings-on while you were here.' With Gosse gone, there was Henry James to seek out : 'I saw James on Tuesday, and he thought the world in general rather a poor affair. He asked affectionately, however, about you, and said how much he had enjoyed his Parisian glimpses of you. Then he gave me a copy of his last volume of tales, forbearing to add, "A poor thing, but me own." Indeed, he couldn't have said that truthfully, for the stories are extremely remarkable – amongst the best that he has done.' Attempting to prolong the memory of his pleasant adventures with Gosse, Harland concludes his letter : '. . . to-night I am to get my grub at the Banquet de la Plume, where Verlaine will preside. I wish you could see the card of invitation – it is very droll and symbolistic, adorned with caricatures of Verlaine and Mallarmé.'[20]

Writing from Paris, James informed Gosse of time spent with Harland : his letter reveals James's awareness of Harland's desperate yearning as a writer :

> Poor Harland came and spent 2 or 3 hours with me the other afternoon – at a café front and on chairs in the Champs-Elysées. He looked better than the time previous, but not well ; and I am afraid things are not too well *with* him. One would like to help him – and I try to – in talk ; but he is not too helpable, for there is a chasm too deep to bridge, I fear, in the pitfall of his literary longings unaccompanied by the *faculty*.[21]

Early in May, James left Paris, which Harland, in a letter to Gosse, described as 'a deserted village' : 'He has gone to Switzerland, whence he writes to tell us that the mountains are *not* poor affairs, and that the Lake of Lucerne is a marvel.'22

The state of Harland's mind in May of 1893 may be discerned from a lengthy letter to Stedman written while he was still in Paris.23 He writes of his distress over repeated rejections of stories by editors of American magazines; he must 'resign' himself to the newspaper syndicates, which mangle his manuscripts and change his titles. In England, however, he fares better, and in London he is welcome in the best periodicals and the best clubs ('. . . in New York I am not good enough for the good periodicals, and the good clubs are above my flight'). But, Harland writes, there are deeper reasons for his preference of London:

> . . . there are reasons of culture, of sentiment; reasons that refer to Art, to Literature, to Human Nature, which I should have to write a volume to establish. . . . But this much is certain – if they would make you Emperor over there, we would come like a shot, and never leave again. If *your* spirit were the spirit of the country and the people, America would be a Paradise on Earth.

Assuring Stedman that he is busily at work, Harland reveals, once again, his disillusionment with the novel as a literary *genre:* 'I don't think I shall ever write a novel again. I don't think the form an especially good, an especially artistic one – and besides, I have never been able to sustain myself through the length of a novel.' Little did Harland know at this time, when his strength was limited and when his short stories were being widely accepted ('When I send my MSS. to English editors, they never come back')24 that his greatest successes were yet to come with the publication of his last novels.

While still in Paris, a major problem that Harland faced was the sudden financial failure of Lovell, the American publisher, who had been prepared to distribute *Mademoiselle Miss*, a collection of short stories. Harland's immediate loss was £100, payable upon publication. Heinemann, the English publisher handling the English edition, went immediately to New York, as Harland wrote to Stedman in his lengthy letter of May 22, 1893, 'to try to save something from the wreck.' Despite these financial and business anxieties, Harland managed to enjoy Paris with 'a host of London friends' who had just arrived, and the 'last fortnight has accordingly been for me a round of gaieties.'

Having decided to remain in France for the summer, the Harlands, with six young English painters, rented a little house in Normandy in the village of Varengeville, near Dieppe. These 'friends, or friends of friends,' as Aline wrote to Stedman in August, included Charles Conder, 'a real genius if ever there was one, a modern Constable'; D. S. MacColl, the art critic, whose water-colours were to be exhibited that autumn in London; and Alfred Thornton, who, like MacColl, wrote a memoir of the episode.[25] The earliest contingent of this group – MacColl, Thornton, and Harland – arrived in early July, wearing blouses and berets, 'the wonder of Dieppe.'[26] Of Harland, MacColl wrote to his sister: 'Harland . . . believes in the "light touch" and "a peculiar quality." He spends his mornings in an attic in a large Jaeger dressing-gown and writes his stories before washing himself. At other moments he lights little bon-fires on the garden walks and cooks potatoes by himself.'[27]

Aline, who managed the house, sat as a model for the painters; in the late afternoon, they all met for tea in the orchard near an inn, not far from their rented house, to discuss art. As Aline described the day's events to Stedman, 'Every night we have music, dancing, and song – in fact our miscellaneous evenings are much recherchés.'[28] The general mood was indeed festive as well as creative. For their own amusement, they acted out a mystery play, *The Garden of Eden*, in which Aline played God, Conder was Adam, and

MacColl, as the serpent, hung enticingly from a tree. At the end of the summer, MacColl wrote a long poem characterizing the residents of the 'festive GROB,' the name of the cottage derived from one of the group, Litellus Goold, and three young sisters named Robinson, who visited them. Of Harland, MacColl wrote:

> 'ARLAND, a most reclusive gent,
> On literary toils intent;
> Yet would he, o'er the flowing bowl,
> Discourse of Nature and the Soul,
> And things less fit for the reporter,
> For half of him was Latin Quarter.[29]

Of major significance in his memoir, however, is MacColl's statement that it was he who suggested to the group 'that what was wanted was a periodical composed of literature and of art independently.' This idea, according to MacColl, was later taken by Harland to John Lane, the publisher, and *The Yellow Book* was born.

In her long letter to Stedman concerning life at the GROB, Aline reveals a new direction in Harland's writing, which she suggests is directly related to his prior illness. It is a striking insight on her part, borne out by the direction of Harland's writing for the remainder of his career:

> Since his illness, which has been far more grave than any one has suspected except his mother and me, his work and he have passed into another Arcana, a more sublimated one, a less flesh and blood one; a more rarefied atmosphere surrounds them. The tragedies are those passing in a conscience, the sensitivenesses of intensely sensitive apprehensions and perceptions. I think that Harry's work will never be popular again, for this reason — but on the other hand it already takes a high literary standing here.[30]

The passage is Jamesian, a reflection of Harland's boundless admiration for the Master. Aline's belief that her husband's work would never again be popular was, of course, mistaken, for Harland, unable to be the true Jamesian disciple, often lapsed into romantic sentimentality, which appealed to a wide audience. Vincent O'Sullivan called him 'a sort of lemonade Henry James.' (*Opinions*, London, 1959, p. 194).

In the autumn of 1893, *Mademoiselle Miss* finally appeared. Consisting of five stories, the volume reveals the new direction of Harland's prose: sensationalism is avoided, but a strongly romantic impulse is apparent. In the opening story, which gives the volume its title, Harland's characteristic infatuation with the images of the Latin Quarter, an American's sentimentalizing of *la vie de Bohème*, results in numerous allusions to the 'Boul Mich', the Luxembourg Gardens, the Rat Mort, the Moulin Rouge, the Chat Noir, and Aristide Bruant's Cabaret du Mirliton – all of which provide settings for the carefree life of art students living in a *pension*. Indeed, Bruant himself appears in one scene at the Mirliton and talks to the students.

In general, however, the stories suffer from a lack of dramatic structure or subtle psychological insight; too often, Harland is merely obvious in his ironies. In 'A Sleeveless Errand,' for example, an American artist, who has succeeded in Paris, returns to visit his boyhood sweetheart after twenty years. To his distress, she has changed considerably, not only physically but also, apparently, in her tactfulness, for she impulsively reacts to his own changed appearance: 'Why, you're as gray as a rat.' Aware that she 'had never existed outside of his imagination,' he decides to see a girl in Minnesota whom he had met on the ship en route to America. Thus, the story ends.

A major event in Harland's life was, to be sure, the editing of *The Yellow Book*, and a major preoccupation ever since has been an accounting of the events that led to the publication of that periodical. As noted already, MacColl writing some forty-five years after the event, recalled that he had mentioned, in Harland's presence, the need for a periodical that would include both art and literature. There is no reason to believe that MacColl's memory was defective, nor is there reason to believe that, during the early nineties, there were not many such suggestions in the air.[31] In any event, the idea captured Harland's imagination, and he asked Aubrey Beardsley if he were interested in associating himself with such a publication.

Harland had met Beardsley, so the story goes, in the waiting room of the latter's physician, Dr. Symes Thompson, and Beardsley probably visited the Harlands in Normandy in the summer of 1893.[32] Whether he stayed at the GROB is unknown (neither MacColl nor Thornton mentions a visit in their memoirs), but by the end of 1893, at the time of Verlaine's visit to London, Beardsley was one of the intimate circle invited to the Harland's Cromwell Road flat to meet the French Decadent.[33] The opportunity to establish a major periodical excited Beardsley, then only twenty-one (Harland was thirty-two), and the two approached John Lane of the Bodley Head with the idea. The event was later described by Harland, in his fanciful way, to an interviewer for the *New York Herald* in 1903. It was on January 1, 1894, a dreary day; 'one of the densest and soupiest and yellowest of all London's infernalest yellow fogs' lay over the city, when Beardsley came to lunch with Harland in the Cromwell Road:

> Aubrey Beardsley and I sat together the whole afternoon before a beautiful glowing open coal fire and I assure you we could scarcely see our hands before our faces with all the candles lighted, for the fog, you know. . . . We declared to each other that we thought it quite a pity and a shame that London publishers should feel themselves longer under obligation to refuse any more of our good manuscripts. . . .

'Tis monstrous, Aubrey,' I said.

'Tis a public scandal,' said he. And then and there we decided to have a magazine of our own. As the sole editorial staff we would feel free and welcome to publish any and all of ourselves that nobody else could be hired to print . . . the next day we had an appointment with Mr John Lane.[34]

The date given by Harland may have been slightly wrong, or Max Beerbohm, visiting Beardsley on January 1, 1894, may have anticipated that Lane would accept the idea, for Max, writing to Reggie Turner on that day, added in a postscript, 'John Lane is just going to start a quarterly magazine called *The Yellow Book* with Harland as Editor and Aubrey as Art Editor. It is to make all our fortunes. . . .'[35]

Arthur Waugh, by his own account, claims to have been 'at the very birth of *The Yellow Book*' on January 3, when, by chance, he was lunching at the National Club in Whitehall Gardens.[36] Harland and Lane had come there to tell Gosse about the new periodical, and Waugh made that meeting the subject of a 'London Letter,' dated January 4, which he sent to *The Critic*.[37] The important point that Waugh makes in his letter concerns the intent of the publisher: *The Yellow Book* was not to be the organ of the Decadence or, indeed, of any 'new movement.' The quarterly would treat 'not of the passing moment and its interests, but (in so far as it deals in criticism at all) with the permanent and stable.' It would contain short stories by 'recognised masters of the craft, poems by "bards approved," and illustrations by "distinguished artists."' Finally, 'an attempt will be made to make the first number thoroughly representative of the most cultured work which is now being done in English literature.' In announcing its literary editor, Waugh states that Harland 'has a large acquaintance with the most conspicuous men of letters of his own day, and a thorough knowledge of the classics of both English and French literature. Moreover, he has unbounded enthusiasm and energy, and is safe to throw himself into the scheme with indomitable interest.'

Clearly, then, neither Harland nor Beardsley believed that *The Yellow Book* was launching a new movement. If it stood for anything, it was, as Waugh was later to state, against 'dullness and incapacity' and 'with no hall-mark except that of excellence.'[38] Privately, Beardsley was willing to go somewhat further. In a letter to Robert Ross, early in January, 1894, he explained : 'Our idea is that many brilliant story painters and picture writers cannot get their best stuff accepted in the conventional magazines, either because they are not topical or perhaps a little risqué.'[39] But, as we shall see, both Harland and Lane were careful to include a broad spectrum of literary and artistic work that made *The Yellow Book* 'representative' of its time.[40]

CHAPTER FOUR

Editing The Yellow Book (1894-1897)

O NCE THE PROPOSAL for *The Yellow Book* was accepted and the title established,[1] the question of contributors was central. According to Waugh, Harland, who was in a 'great state of excitement' that day when he and Lane met with Gosse early in 1894, began listing names:

> He would have Henry James and George Saintsbury; of course Gosse must come in; and how about Dr. Garnett? That would be a sound bodyguard of the old brigade. Then, of the new school, Hubert Crackanthorpe was indispensable; and they must have Arthur Symons. And Lane put in a word for William Watson; and Gosse asked, Why not Arthur Christopher Benson? And Harland agreed, Why not indeed?[2]

Harland's mention of James's name first indicates his devotion to the Master. Indeed, Harland and Beardsley, after *The Yellow Book* was established, called upon James at 34 De Vere Gardens, not far from Harland's flat, to solicit a contribution to the first number. As James described the visit: 'I was invited, and all urgently, to contribute to the first number, and was regaled with the golden truth that my composition might absolutely assume, might shamelessly parade in, its own organic form.'[3] Indeed, James was pleased that Harland would permit him as much space as he wished and needed. James's contribution, 'The Death of the Lion,' was given the honour of the first of the 'Letterpress' selections in the inaugural volume. Contributions by Saintsbury, Watson, Dr. Garnett, Benson, and Gosse, all mentioned by Waugh in reporting the plans for the first volume, also appeared, calculated, presumably, to balance the more daring contributions by Symons, a poem titled 'Stella Maris,' not about the Virgin, as the title might imply, but about a prostitute ; the ironic mockery of Max Beerbohm's 'A Defence of Cosmetics,' and, of course, Beardsley's illustrations. Other selections, reflecting the current French naturalism as well as the Romantic revival, were also included. Crackanthorpe's 'Modern Melodrama' depicts the death of a woman afflicted by an incurable disease, and Ella D'Arcy's 'Irremediable' tells the story of a misalliance between a sensitive man and a commonplace woman, one of a number of stories in *The Yellow Book* concerned with bad marriages.

Ella D'Arcy, quite unknown before her appearance in the periodical, was called 'Assistant Editor' by J. Lewis May in his *John Lane and the Nineties*, but she denied that she had an official position : 'I was around a good bit, and helped as I could. But I never was really an editor.'[4] However, Harland referred to her as 'the Sub-Editor of the *Yellow Book*' in a letter of recommendation to Dr. Richard Garnett, then Keeper of Books at the British Museum, to whom she was applying for a position,[5] and in a letter to Lane, Harland also referred to her as his 'Sub-Editor.'[6] Harland, who regarded her as a 'remarkable' discovery for *The Yellow Book*,[7] met her early in 1894, when, briefly out of London, he stopped for a day at Hythe to see her 'in the flesh,' as he wrote to Richard Le Gallienne : 'She is interesting-looking, very good-natured, and most intelligent, though perhaps a trifle inclined to take things somewhat too seriously in this least serious of possible worlds.'[8] Interestingly, Ella D'Arcy, in later years, thought that what Harland 'lacked was a serious purpose in life. But he insisted always on being light-minded and amusing.'[9]

Apparently, the serious D'Arcy and the light-minded Harland got on well together : Harland accepted ten of her stories for *The Yellow Book's* thirteen issues, and they translated Dauphin Meunier's article on Madame Réjane for the July, 1894 issue.[10] The demise of *The Yellow Book*, however, substantially ended the brilliant promise of her literary career, and apparently Harland and she had little contact in the years following.

Despite Harland's pose as a frivolous, charming wit, he was in deadly earnest about his role as literary editor of *The Yellow Book*. His letters to Lane in the Westfield College archive reveal a determined editor who would, if necessary, pay contributors out of his own pocket to attract the best writers. In addition, he had to reassure Lane, on many occasions, that the fees paid to contributors were not excessive. In a letter written on June 15, 1894, for example, Harland, after listing in considerable detail what he planned to pay contributors to the second issue, concludes :

> If you will ask any Editor in England what he thinks would be a fair average price per page for literary matter of the standard published in the *Yellow Book*, he will tell you at the lowest 15 shillings. Yet I am getting you 300 pages, all the stuff good, much of it coming from men of high rank, at the rate 13/4 a page ; that is £2 for every three pages, and as our page contains about 350 words, that is under £2 a thousand.'

The lowest average price per thousand words, Harland wrote to Lane, 'you can possibly count upon getting good stuff for is £2 : 2 : 0.' In this same letter, filled with details on payments to individual writers for their contributions to the second volume, Harland advises Lane to 'risk another £50' to secure certain contributors : 'If I had the money, I would risk it myself ; but I happen for the moment to be hard up.'

Harland proposed that he would lend Lane whatever money was owed to him for his editorial work on the first volume to ensure that the £50 would go to the second volume:

> That shows how thoroughly in earnest I am, how thoroughly I believe in the *Y.B.*, and how anxious I am to see its contents as strong as they can be made. I have as yet not made one penny by it, and you know whether I have worked hard for it. Not only have I made nothing by it, but I have paid out no end of shillings for postage and stationery, and I pay Miss D'Arcy as sub-Editor from my own pocket. Yet rather than see the list of Vol. II weakened, I offer to lend you all that may be due to me on Vol. I, provided you will put up £50 more.

Somehow, Harland was able, on occasion, to secure contributions without payment,[11] and on at least one occasion, he offered one of his own stories without payment. In citing items for the second volume, he wrote in his June 15 letter to Lane:

> Henry Harland. He gives his story for the love of the *Y.B.*, though the *Idler* pays him £3 : 3 : 0 a thousand words ; and the *New Review* pays him £2 : 2 : 0.

Despite the small financial rewards for his work on *The Yellow Book*, Harland's devotion to the periodical was unaffected, for he sensed its importance as perhaps the most significant literary event of the early 1890s, and he wished it to be a major force in English letters and art.

The only periodical that had previously approached *The Yellow Book* in importance was *The Century Guild Hobby Horse*, but, as James G. Nelson has stated, 'no magazine with such high and uncommercial aims had hitherto been planned for a wide audience,'[12] and in its announced intention of dealing entirely with art and literature (avoiding the customary political and social topics and the book reviews found in the conventional periodical), it was unique at the time. In addition, its aesthetic appearance was quite strikingly different from the commercial magazines. In the first place, it was bound as a book, but, more important, as Nelson writes, 'In keeping with the ideals of the Revival of Printing, the magazine was printed entirely in Caslon old-face type. Not only was the title page, like those Beardsley designed for *Keynotes* and *The Dancing Faun*, strikingly different from the weak, crowded, unaesthetic title pages of the usual Victorian journal, but the typography of each essay began in a new and attractive way.'[13] Moreover, a catchword was added to each page, and 'fly-titles' preceded each plate.

As an editor, Harland had good journalistic sense in presenting dramatic confrontations between differing points of view and in balancing the conventional with the *avant-garde*. For the first issue, he accepted Waugh's 'Reticence in Literature,' advocating with characteristic Victorian prudence, restraint in the presentation of unusual subjects (the implication, of course, was that sexuality must never be explicit). In accepting the essay, Harland immediately saw that interest could be provoked by opposing such a view in the next issue; consequently, he wrote to Waugh: 'Your article is altogether delightful, and the *Yellow Book* will take joy in enclosing it. Of course I don't agree with all of your argument, but it is all charmingly stated. Perhaps (if you don't mind) I will ask some advocate of the other side, to write a rejoinder, to appear in Volume II.'[14] Subsequently, Harland published Crackanthorpe's response to Waugh's essay. He also published 'A Letter to the Editor' by Max Beerbohm in the second volume criticizing those critics who had attacked his essay, 'A Defence of Cosmetics,' and thus extending the ironies that the critics had missed.

Nor was Harland reluctant to include his own stories and criticism in *The Yellow Book*. For the first volume, he included two of his 'sketches': 'Mercedes' and 'A Broken Looking-Glass,' both reprinted in *Grey Roses* (1895). The second sketch, the more important of the two, is Proustian in its use of involuntary memory, the device being a looking glass, that recalls to a dying writer's mind the dead girl that he had loved (her mother had given it to him). In his wish to recapture the past by looking into the glass, the writer allows it to slip from his hand, and it shatters. He is found dead, the symbolic looking glass at his side. It is a sensitive story of lost images and shattered dreams, Joycean in its elegiac mood and symbolic technique.

Possibly because Harland was a novelist and also a short story writer, the literary contents of *The Yellow Book*, in most of its volumes, are more distinguished by its prose than by its verse. The late nineteenth century, however, was deeply interested in the possibility of prose as a fine art, principally because of the influence of Walter Pater, whose writings pointed in that direction. One of Pater's professed disciples, Richard Le Gallienne, was later to write that prose 'seemed, so to say, to have more future than verse ; less had been done with it ; and many young pundits declared it the great art of the two. What solemn talks I have heard on the subject in the elaborate periods of Oscar Wilde and in the vivacious whimsical harangues of Henry Harland !'[15] And Le Gallienne gives a vivid impression of Harland at work :

> The polishing of his prose was for him his being's end and aim, and I have often seen him at that sacred task of a forenoon, in his study-bedroom, still in pyjamas and dressing-gown, with a coffee-pot on the hearth, bending over an exquisite piece of hand-writing, like a gold-smith at his bench. It was his theory that the brain was freshest immediately after rising, and he was jealous of dissipating that morning energy by any activities of the toilet, leaving his bath and his breakfast, which with him, of course, was *déjeuner*, till the real business of the day, a page of 'perfect prose,' was accomplished.[16]

Le Gallienne's notion that Harland was devoted to the 'sacred task' of creating an imperishable work of art, suggesting a devotion to the Religion of Art, is also stated by Aline

Harland, who, in a letter to Stedman, explains that 'nothing really matters but art – and our experiences human are as nothing till they have uttered themselves in some of the Beauty which you and Harry and a few others worship.'[17] According to a reported conversation, however, Wilde was less inclined to be reverential towards Harland's devotion to his prose, for when Harland once told him that he was 'fairly nauseated' over his own work by the time he completed it, Wilde replied : 'I should think you would be.'[18]

Harland's presumed preference for prose over poetry has been attributed by some critics to his dislike of the latter. However, Harland was, in his early career, an admirer of Browning, for whose works high praise is expressed in the 'Sidney Luska' novels. In *The Yoke of the Thorah*, for example, Elias, praising *Inn Album* and *The Ring and the Book*, exclaims :

> When I read Browning, the exhilaration was almost physical. It was like breathing some vivifying atmosphere, like drinking some powerful elixir. It made me glow and tingle through and through. It was as though the very inmost quick of my spirit had been touched and made to throb and thrill. . . . No music, not even Beethoven's or Wagner's, ever moved me, ever carried me away as these poems of Browning's did. They literally transfixed me, magnetized me, like the spell of a magician.[19]

In 1893, Harland's only published poem, 'The King's Touch,' a lengthy work of ninety-five lines clearly influenced by Browning, appeared in *Liber Scriptorum*, a leather-bound volume containing contributions by 190 members of the Authors Club of New York.[20] The poem reveals Harland's slender talent as a versifier, but what is interesting is his depiction of masks (no doubt following Browning) in the image of a villain who has been ennobled by the touch of Death :

To us he had unmasked himself, and shown
His devil's visage and his cloven hoof.

The speaker, accepting the sanctity of all human life, is deeply
affected by the mysterious nature of the villain's transformation in death :

Because we knew his whole life's infamy,
Now wear grave faces, speak with bated breath,
Are awe-struck, sobered, filled with mysterious fear,
Name his name solemnly, and salute his bier.

It is apparently this poem that Harland showed to Le Gallienne
for an opinion, possibly with an eye to reprinting it. Le Gallienne's critique has not survived, but Harland wrote to him
on *The Yellow Book* stationery : 'I am glad my poor doggerel
strikes you as not altogether bad, but I can't convince myself
that it is worth reprinting. Let it lie − in peace, in its £20
sepulchre. And no, I shall try my hand at no more verse. I
have no real "vocation" in that galley, and besides, prose
tempts me more. Oh, I would give five fingers to be able to
accomplish one perfect bit of prose.'[21]

In his capacity as editor, Harland revealed his critical
sense and interest in poetry by the revisions he suggested to
his contributors. He clearly did not accept poetry grudgingly
for *The Yellow Book*, as his letters to Lane reveal. For example,
in the autumn of 1894, Harland outlined the contents of
Volume IV (January, 1895) in a letter to Lane : 'Le Gallienne
is going to give us his sonnet "Home," instead of prose, this
time. We will lead off with it, and as it's a very fine composition, it will do him and us good.' What follows in an interesting afterthought but not, I believe, an indication that
payments and space preceded considerations of quality : 'It
will also save us 19 pages, and £25, as he says he will accept
no payment for it.'[22]

Little is known of how Harland and Beardsley worked
together on *The Yellow Book*, insofar as selection of material

is concerned. The published Beardsley letters reveal nothing of their collaboration – if, indeed, they did consult each other – and Harland's letters to Lane rarely mention Beardsley or the illustrations for the various volumes. A rare instance occurs in a postcard to Lane – unusual for its expression of impatience – in which Harland writes : *'Why doesn't* Aubrey send me his list? Impossible to paginate without it.'[23] Harland puts four lines under the first two words to emphasize the urgency. Lane was personally involved with both the literary and artistic contents and presumably maintained peace between the two editors so that neither the literary nor the artistic selections encroached upon the other. Indeed, as the correspondence in the Lane Archive at Westfield College indicates, contributors often submitted material directly to Lane rather than to Harland or Beardsley. Harland, of course, was often abroad for his health, but even when he was in London, Lane took an editorial hand in the selection of material. For example, when Lane arranged to have James do an article for the twelfth volume (January, 1897) on George Sand and Musset, Harland wrote : 'James will do the article for ten guineas, and have it finished by the end of next week. *You were* clever to arrange it. I think it will do the book vast good.'[24] According to his own account, Lane was perpetually anxious about Beardsley's illustrations, for any one of them might conceal phallic symbols cleverly disguised for the amusement of friends, and he would have to examine them carefully and 'look at them upside down.'[25] Like Harland, Lane was concerned about balancing the conventional with the daring, and hence made certain that Sir Frederick Leighton's neo-classical drawing, 'A Study,' followed Beardsley's illustrations for the cover and title page of Volume I.

In early April, 1894, announcements were sent out by the Bodley Head of the forthcoming appearance of *The Yellow*

Book, and on April 13, Waugh sent his 'London Letter' to *The Critic*, informing his American readers that on Monday, April 16, the periodical would be published and on that evening the editors and contributors, supported by their wives and friends, would dine together at a little hotel in Soho to 'inaugurate' the periodical's 'new career' : 'Meanwhile, the new quarterly is on many lips ; the editors are being liberally interviewed ; and everything looks rosy for the first appearance.'[26]

The day of publication arrived, and bookstores in the Charing Cross Road took on a distinctly yellow hue. The most dazzling spectacle of all was in the little bow window of the Bodley Head, where Frederick Chapman, Lane's manager, gave the youthful J. Lewis May a lesson in window display, 'creating such a mighty glow of yellow at the far end of Vigo Street that one might have been forgiven for imagining for a moment that some awful portent had happened, and that the sun had risen in the West.'[27] In the first weeks, the public demand for copies was overwhelming. In May, Aline Harland, apologizing to Stedman for Lane's failure to send him a copy, wrote that 'the first three weeks of its appearance there was such a rush upon the book that the London and out of town booksellers could not be supplied fast enough. . . .'[28]

On the evening of April 16, *The Yellow Book* dinner took place at the Hotel d'Italie in Old Compton Street, an event reported on by Waugh for *The Critic*.[29] Harland's 'magnetic influence' pervaded the room, and he was everywhere, introducing everyone to everyone and radiating good spirits. Mrs Elizabeth Pennell sat between him and Beardsley in the 'seat of honor' ; Dr. Richard Garnett, 'sole representative of the older school,' sat in a corner ; George Moore and John Oliver Hobbes, who had collaborated on the first act of a play, *The Fool's Hour*, in the inaugural volume, sat together. Not far away sat Theo Marzials, 'comparing the poets of his youth with the poets of to-day' ; opposite him sat Yeats, 'whose earnest, clean-shaven face gave an air of seriousness to his corner.' Next to him sat his friend, the youthful Lionel Johnson, and close by sat Walter Sickert, the 'wit of the evening.' Others present were the poet John Davidson, Ernest Rhys (with his wife), Ernest Dowson, and Max Beerbohm. Notable absentees were Henry James, who was abroad ;[30] Gosse, who was ill but who sent 'a copy of delightful verses to represent him' ; Arthur Symons and Hubert Crackanthorpe, both in Italy ; and Richard Le Gallienne, who was in Liverpool to deliver a lecture.

Adding further details to this notable evening in his later memoirs, Waugh wrote that Olivia Shakespear, a cousin of Lionel Johnson, spent much time with George Moore and his collaborator. Waugh also mentions an amusing speech by Sickert, who looked forward to a time when authors would be compelled to write stories and poems around pictures, an idea directly antithetical to the policy of *The Yellow Book*.[31]

The account of the dinner given by Elizabeth Pennell, who sat between Harland and Beardsley, is markedly different in some detail from that given by Waugh. According to Mrs Pennell, Harland and Beardsley had consulted her husband, Joseph Pennell, the artist and critic, about establishing *The Yellow Book*: 'They begged for ideas, begged for contributions. He rather laughed at the qualifications of these inexperienced art and literary editors, but he made suggestions out of his unfailing supply and let them have the etching of Le Puy for a full-page reproduction.'[32] Because Pennell was abroad at the time of *The Yellow Book* dinner, the editors invited Mrs Pennell to occupy the 'seat of honour between them at the high table.' But instead of entertaining her with spirited talk, they ignored her, she wrote, while all about there was gaiety and laughter : 'They were both as nervous as débutantes at a first party. Shrinking from the shadow cast before by their coming speeches, neither of them had as much as a word to throw me' (See *Nights* p.186). However, when they gave their speeches, the 'strain' eased, and apparently Mrs Pennell became the centre of attention.

One of the speeches at the dinner was given by John Lane on behalf of the Bodley Head, but Elkin Mathews was not present. Why he did not attend is explained at great length in a letter to Dr. T. N. Brushfield, physician, author, and antiquarian, in which Mathews gives a history of how he and Lane had reached the breaking point in their relationship, resulting in the dissolution of their partnership in the autumn of 1894. With obvious anger, Mathews says of Lane that he 'falsifies matters as is his custom whenever it suits him to do so,' that Lane was 'an impossible man to get on with – a man who was simply working for his own hand.' Then, pointing to *The Yellow Book* dinner, Mathews implies that Lane's behaviour was the beginning of the end of their partnership :

> But the climax came when the Editors of the *Yellow Book* gave a dinner to the contributors & Lane alone represented the firm. I only heard about this dinner by accident – Lane never volunteered any information about it until I taxed him.
>
> I learned afterwards that many enquired where *I* was – and that when Lane was asked to speak for the publishers – he with the boldest effrontery said that he deeply regretted the *unavoidable* absence of his partner – and that he was not present to join in the general enthusiasm & so on.
>
> As a matter of fact I could have attended the dinner with the greatest ease in the world. I had *absolute* leisure that evening, and there was not the slightest colour for him to make such a statement.
>
> He had evidently represented to the Editors that he alone was the partner interested in the working of the *Yellow Book*, and they did not take the trouble to act otherwise. I heard that when Lane expressed his

regret at my 'unavoidable' absence, one prominent author shouted out 'That [is] a lie.'[33]

Mathews, however, permitted Lane to manage the business and editorial end of *The Yellow Book* perhaps out of a sense that Lane had wanted to direct it in his own way and would brook no interference from his partner.

The critical reception of *The Yellow Book* on both sides of the Atlantic, now celebrated as one of the most extra-ordinary episodes of abuse in literary history, need not again be rehearsed here. However, one review, in *The Speaker*,[34] may be cited, since it roused Harland's ire. The reviewer imagines Lane and Mathews saying 'to the band of Bodley Head disciples' : 'Be mystic, be weird, be precious, be advanced, be without value.' And citing contributions by Crackanthorpe, George Egerton, and Harland, the reviewer comments : 'The three of them seem, if the metaphor may be permitted, like men who should carve at a feather-pillow with knives in order to make of it a statue.' Distressed by the notice, Harland wrote to Lane : 'We are frightfully abused in *The Speaker*. I am half inclined to think the article libellous — in which case we could make them apologise or pay damages.'[35] But no doubt Lane urged Harland to take such abuse in his stride (perhaps even pointing out to him that a *succès de scandale* was better for sales than stony silence) ; in any event, Harland did not press the matter. But in the same letter, he reveals his concern about the critical reception of the first volume — particularly in the singling out of his co-editor's illustrations: 'Aubrey must modify himself in Vol. II.' Beardsley, however, was delighted by the critical attention, even if much of it was abusive. To Henry James, he wrote : 'Have you heard of the storm that raged over No. 1 ? Most of the thunderbolts fell on my head. However, I enjoyed the excitement immensely.'[36]

But some contributors to *The Yellow Book* were not

pleased to be associated with the periodical, perhaps because of its yellowish appearance or its critical reception. James, who had been urged to contribute to the second volume by Harland, was at work on 'The Coxon Fund' but clearly regretted being associated with the publication (though he continued to contribute to it). In a letter from Rome on May 28, 1894, he wrote to his brother, William :

> I haven't sent you *The Yellow Book* — on purpose ; and I have been weeks and weeks receiving a copy of it myself. I say on purpose because although my little tale which ushers it in ('The Death of the Lion') appears to have had, for a thing of mine, an unusual success, I hate too much the horrid aspect and company of the whole publication. And yet I am again to be intimately, conspicuously associated with the 2nd number. It is for gold and to oblige the worshipful Harland (the editor).[37]

When Harland invited Mrs Pearl Craigie, who, as 'John Oliver Hobbes,' had contributed with Moore the first act of a play, never completed, to the first volume, she wrote to Moore : '[Harland] wants me to write a poem, story, an article, anything, for the next number. I fear I cannot oblige him. *The Speaker* on *The Yellow Book* is only too just. I have never seen such a vulgar production.'[38] And when Katherine Bradley and Edith Cooper ('Michael Field'), first saw the volumes of *The Yellow Book* displayed in the windows of the Bodley Head, they were 'almost blinded by the glare of hell.'[39]

Regardless of such adverse reactions to *The Yellow Book*, Harland was now a major figure in the literary world of the 1890s who could launch the careers of the unknown or lure the illustrious to the pages of the most talked-about periodical in London. He welcomed new talent; indeed, many of the issues contain stories and poems by writers — many of them women — never before published, and he took pleasure in his new discoveries. After the appearance of Volume I, when he received an unsolicited manuscript in the mail, he wrote to Lane : 'By post, from an entirely unknown person, a Miss [Charlotte] Mew, I have received one of the most remarkable MSS. I have ever read. A story, most subtle and imaginative, and done in a wonderful original style. A new *Y.B.* discovery – fully as remarkable as Ella D'Arcy, though in a totally different way.'[40] The story, titled 'Passed,' which appeared in the second volume in July, depicts the strange experiences of a narrator, who, expressing herself in a highly metaphorical and allegorical manner, witnesses poverty, death, and the religious experience.

In May, 1894, a month after the appearance of Volume I, the Harlands left London for Paris to escape from the unpleasantness of the attacks on *The Yellow Book*. Aline's important letter to Stedman, written from Paris, reveals Harland's distress not only at the review in *The Speaker* but also at the general abuse at the hands of the critics (significantly, Aline, who shared her husband's public life so intimately, uses the editorial 'we') :

> As we have succeeded in spite of their unfriend-
> liness we bear them only the slight grudge and small
> amount of contempt one cannot help feeling for mean-
> ness unspeakable, and we hope with Heaven's help to
> succeed so much better in our second number, even than
> in our first, that they will be the laughing stock of the
> public and *The Yellow Book*. It is impossible to tell you
> the bitterness, hatred and malice rife in the London art
> world – how each big fish lives by devouring the little
> fishes as fast as they become half big enough to hold
> their own. It is all so heart-sickening that we are glad
> to get away from London and out of it all for a fortnight,
> when we shall be obliged to go back again & face the
> world and the devil a second time.[41]

In June, Harland returned to London to prepare the

second volume, due in July, for the printer, while Aline remained in Paris. In deciding on the contents, he found that the cost of the literary selections would exceed the allotted £200 for fees to contributors, despite the fact that he and Beerbohm would not receive payment. The illustrations, he informed Lane, would be no less than £50:

> I shall have to cut out £50 worth from the literary contents or you will have to pay separately for the pictures. The former alternative would be a pity, for it would greatly weaken the number, especially as to spare the £50 I should have to cut out some of the best names, and hold their contributions over for Vol. III. You see, in Vol. I, people worked for low prices because we were an experiment, but now everyone expects his full usual scale of payment.'[42]

Harland concludes by reassuring Lane that cost per page has been kept low: 'Please note that the list runs to 300 pages. £200 for 300pp. makes less than 14 shillings a page.'

For the second volume, according to Lane, Harland wrote to Andrew Lang inviting him to write a critique of Volume I. Lang, however, 'indignantly refused.' The idea apparently originated with Lane, who, in preparing notes for his *Aubrey Beardsley and the Yellow Book* (1903), wrote:

> The papers, particularly *The Times*, slanged the Quarterly so much that I felt it was imperative to get some staid critic to criticise, and, if possible, slog the first volume, and I went to France myself and arranged with P. G. Hamerton, who had then just retired from the editorship of his art journal, to write a criticism. To our dismay, he wrote nothing but appreciation.[43]

Hamerton's critique, however, does not uniformly praise Volume I. In discussing Symons' 'Stella Maris,' for example, Hamerton regrets its publication, for its title and subject matter are offensive. 'Why,' he asks, 'should poetic art be employed to celebrate common fornication?'[44]

Harland's contribution, a story titled 'A Responsibility,' is an attempt at a tale in the Jamesian manner of an opportunity lost by the narrator, who insensitively discourages friendship on the part of a younger man and who regrets his action after the other's suicide. The volume also includes John Davidson's poem, 'Thirty Bob a Week,' which T. S. Eliot was later to praise highly; an essay by Crackanthorpe replying to Waugh's 'Reticence in Literature' and praising the New Realism; and concluding the volume, as he had opened the first, Henry James, who submitted 'The Coxon Fund.' (John Singer Sargent's drawing of James also appeared in the volume.)

Returning to Paris to rejoin Aline, Harland wrote to Le Gallienne to join them 'in this enchanted town, where the sun shines, and the coffee-houses prosper, and everybody has the Artistic Temperament more or less' : 'Aline and I are seated at this moment on the terrace of the Café de la Paix – and I am writing on my knee, which accounts for the tremulousness of my hand. . . . We are drinking iced coffee, because the air is hot ; and such a funny motley crowd is surging backwards and forwards on the pavement – Infidels, Jews, and Turks, as well as Christian English and Parisians – priests, soldiers, bourgeois and prostitutes.'[45] Le Gallienne, intrigued by Harland's promise to 'dine with Dauphin Meunier and sup with dear old Verlaine,' joined the Harlands in Paris. Crackanthorpe came, too, and the party presumably made the rounds of the Symbolist haunts on the 'Boul' Mich' much as Harland and Gosse had done in the previous year. Commemorating the event, Le Gallienne recalled that October in a poem, dedicated to Aline :

Once more, once more, my heart to sit
With Aline's smile and Harry's wit.[46]

Harland's love affair with Paris moved him to occasional rhetorical flights (the analogy of his actual flights in the spring,

75

as much for his health as for his escape from prosaic London). In a letter to Le Gallienne, probably written early in 1894, he lamented that Cromwell Road 'smells of Philistia and the Stock Exchange. When the Spring comes – when the Spring comes! And it will come soon now. In France its touch can be already felt. Violets are blossoming at Nice, and pretty girls are peddling them in the streets of Paris, and before long the new grass will be sprouting in the Bois and the Luxembourg. O, France – O, Paris – O, my heart! If I were a Frenchman, and lived in Paris, I should write verse every year, with the return of Spring.'[47]

Volume III of *The Yellow Book* appeared in October, while Harland was in Paris (he had, presumably, prepared it for the press before leaving to rejoin Aline). The critical reception lacked the abusiveness conferred upon the first volume, but there was little praise for its contents. In America, *The Critic*, continuing its disapproval, entitled its review 'A Yellow Bore' : 'One is beginning to dread the coming around of the quarters of the year. Not because they mark the flight of time, but because they announce the coming of *The Yellow Book*.'[48]

Harland's contribution, 'When I Am King,' the title derived from a song written by its central character, reveals a growing obsession with the theme of the failed artist. The narrator's name, interestingly enough, is Harry, and the composer's name is Pair : could Harland be suggesting, if only unconsciously, that Pair is his feared double? In the story, Harry, en route to Biarritz, stops at a waterfront *brasserie-à-femmes* in Bordeaux and discovers his old friend, Pair, whom he has not seen in fifteen years, playing the piano for dancing harlots and drunken sailors. Unable, despite his genius, to sell his songs, he has, in performing in such an establishment, clearly prostituted himself (one wonders whether Harland, in contemplating his 'Sidney Luska' novels had not thought the same of himself). Again, Harland employs a Proustian device for recapturing the past when Harry, before he discovers Pair's identity, hears the 'obscure old pianist' playing a familiar tune :

A dance had ended,and after a breathing spell he began to play an interlude. It was an instance of how tunes, like perfumes, have the power to wake sleeping memories. The tune he was playing now, simple and dreamy like a lullaby, and strangely at variance with the surroundings, whisked me off in a twinkling, far from the actual – ten, fifteen years backwards – to my student life in Paris and set me to thinking, as I had not thought for many a long day, of my hero, friend and comrade, Edmund Pair. . .[49]

As though he had been reading Hardy, Pair assails his 'ill luck' in attempting to find a suitable position after he could find no publishers for his songs : 'I had ill luck, ill luck, ill luck – nothing but ill luck, defeat, disappointment. Was it the will of Heaven ? I wondered what unforgiveable sin I had committed to be punished so.' The story, however, falls into pathos without the elevating power of Hardy's tragic vision (the result, perhaps, of Harland's too close identification with Pair ?).

Other contributors who had also appeared before in previous issues were Symons, D'Arcy, Beerbohm, Watson, Crackanthorpe, and John Davidson, whose poem, 'The Ballad of a Nun,' tells of a nun who flees a convent, engages in worldly adventures,and returns with little repentance. New to the third volume is Olive Custance, who was to contribute poems to eight of the thirteen volumes ; and Ernest Dowson, represented by a story, 'Apple-Blossom in Brittany.'

Back in London in late 1894 to prepare the fourth volume for the press, Harland was looking forward to spending another spring in Paris, a most momentous spring, for by that time the Wilde arrest would take place and Beardsley would be sacked. Despite his view of the Cromwell Road as philistine, Harland made his flat a mecca for the great and the aspiring. Many memoirs of the 1890s graphically depict Saturday evenings 'at home' with the Harlands. Evelyn Sharp, a novelist and short story writer, who contributed to six issues of *The Yellow Book*, was often there, where she never saw Wilde (who avoided *The Yellow Book* set generally, since Harland, Beardsley, and Lane had agreed to exclude him from its pages) and only rarely saw Beardsley. When James was present, the group sat with 'dumb humility' as he walked up and down the room 'seeking the word he wanted for the completion of his sentence.' It was, writes Sharp, 'an immense honour to have been invited to worship at the shrine; but the atmosphere cleared pleasantly when he left and our editor became himself again.' Convinced that *The Yellow Book* represented a 'genuine Renaissance of art and literature,' Sharp wrote of her evenings with the Harlands: 'Those of us who met at 144 Cromwell Road on Saturday evenings did not care much what conventional society thought of us, so long as we could succeed in pleasing our editor's fastidious taste in letters and avoid the two cardinal sins of banality and insincerity.' The evenings were not, however, devoted entirely to literary talk. Sometimes Aline sang French songs, and sometimes there was instrumental music, but when there was talk, Harland was the 'soul and the inspiration' of the group with his 'endearing and whimsical personality.'[50] But C. Lewis Hind, editor of the *Pall Mall Budget* and later of *The Academy*, wondered, while observing the tubercular Harland and Beardsley on those Saturday evenings, who would die first.[51]

The Harlands, however, were not always a congenial couple, but they were generally 'popular,' as Beerbohm wrote to Robert Ross.[52] According to Netta Syrett, a *Yellow Book* contributor, they were 'erratic' and when bored on Saturday evenings 'made little effort to disguise their feelings.'[53] Once, when Syrett was with the Harlands in Paris, there was disagreement as to which restaurant they would dine in after seeing a play : Harland wanted to go to one place, Aline another. Leading the way, he 'pushed open the doors of the restaurant of *his* choice, and we followed, Aline grumbling all the time. Suddenly enraged, he turned on her with, "*All right, we won't go anywhere at all!*" ' Syrett had to follow 'two angry people' who, 'under the astonished gaze of the waiters and the diners seated at the tables, rushed out of the room they had just entered . . . all three of us went supperless to our beds !'[54]

In January, 1895, the fourth volume appeared, containing many familiar names of contributors whom, by now, readers of the periodical had come to expect. This, also, may be a sign that Harland, either from loyalty to his authors or from his inability to attract really notable writers (not a single major writer is represented in the volume), was relying upon an established, recognizable coterie. This may be a decided strength for a publication ; in this case, however, it was a grave weakness, for there were simply too many minor writers among the contributors. Harland, however, was constantly trying to lure the more important writers, as we have seen in his success with James. To Coventry Patmore, Harland wrote : 'I wish I could persuade you to let the *Yellow Book* have a poem. It would turn red with pride.'[55] But Patmore maintained his distance. Harland also wrote to Alice Meynell, claiming that he had heard that she had 'unbounded enthusiasm' for *The Yellow Book*,[56] but she, too, declined. Francis Thompson followed suit, as did George Meredith. Harland may also have asked Kipling and Hardy ; nothing by them appeared in *The Yellow Book*. Clearly, there was, as we have seen, an aversion in certain circles to the periodical ; as Katherine L. Mix has stated, 'neither gold nor kind words could lure some of London's leading *littérateurs* to the *Yellow Book.*'[57]

At the same time, however, Harland was unwilling to accept submissions from any writers, major or minor, if they were not up to what he regarded as *Yellow Book* standards. In a letter to Lane, Harland wrote on Wells's submissions : 'On two occasions Wells has offered me scientific stories, and neither of them was good – not to be compared to the things of his that I've seen in the *P[all] M[all] G[azette]* and the *New Review*. Of course I should be delighted if he'd send us something of his *best*, but we don't want his or anyone's *second* best.'[58] Of a lesser-known writer, Harland wrote that his story is 'distinctly his *second* best, or even his *third* best. We mustn't let people shove their second and third best wares off on the *Y.B.* It's a perfectly conventional bit of melodrama, that would do well enough in *Black and White* or in the *Strand Magazine*, but is miles below the *Y.B.* standard.'[59]

In March, 1895, after he had arranged the contents that would appear in the April volume, Harland, with Aline, left London for Paris. On April 5, Wilde's libel suit against the Marquess of Queensberry collapsed, and, on the same day, Wilde was arrested at the Cadogan Hotel and ordered to stand trial. The story involving Beardsley's dismissal from *The Yellow Book* because of his previous association with Wilde is too well known to be retold in detail here.[60] In America at the time, Lane permitted the dismissal to take place, because pressure upon him by several Bodley Head authors was too great. He wrote to George Egerton shortly after he arrived in New York, where he read of Wilde's arrest : '. . . I have been terribly worried re Oscar – Beardsley –Yellow Book. I have had no peace since my arrival, nothing but cables (Oh ! the expense of them !).'[61]

Harland was not involved in the decision to fire Beards-

1. Aline Harland, ca. 1890
[From the E. C. Stedman Papers, Columbia University.]

2. John Lane (in the 1890s)
[From the E. C. Stedman Papers, Columbia University.]

3. Beardsley Sketch of Harland, ca. 1894
[From *The Early Works of Aubrey Beardsley* (New York:
Dover Publications, 1967).]

4. Beerbohm Caricature of Harland
[From Max Beerbohm's *Caricature of Twenty-Five Gentlemen* (London:
Leonard Smithers, 1896); rpt. in *Max's Nineties* (London: Rupert Hart-
Davies, 1958).]

5. Henry Harland, ca. 1902
[From *The Critic* (New York), 44 (Feb., 1904), 108. A studio
photograph by Frederick Hollyer, London.]

ley; indeed, he deplored the removal of Beardsley's illustrations from the April volume, remained on good terms with him, and in fact expected him to re-appear in the July number. Writing to Gosse early in May from Paris, Harland informed him that Beardsley had joined him and Aline 'a fortnight ago, and he's capital company. He says he's going back to London and work to-night. . . . Yes, his absence from the *Y.B.* is deplorable : but what is one to do with a capricious boy whose ruling passion is a desire to astonish the public with the unexpected? He'll be in the July number, I hope, larger than ever.'[62] The implication in Harland's letter is that he apparently believed that the omission of Beardsley's illustrations was merely an expediency of the moment and that Beardsley was unaware that he had been fired as art editor. According to Ella D'Arcy, Harland's absence from London was a crucial factor, for had he been at the Bodley Head, 'everything would have been different.'[63]

Harland's health seems to have been worse than he had thought, for he remained in France (mostly in Dieppe) until the autumn. He corresponded with Chapman on *Yellow Book* matters, particularly when the fifth volume, due for publication on April 16, had to be rescheduled for April 30 because of substitutions required for Beardsley's design for the cover and title page (the substitution for the latter is particularly poor, and through some error, Beardsley's design for the back cover remained). Writing from Paris, Harland informed Chapman in mid-April :

> So far as I can gather from Miss D'Arcy's letters, all the sheets will have been passed for press by to-day. I am wiring her to hurry the printers. I don't doubt we shall be out in time, in spite of the awkward interruption of Easter. It is a pity about the title-page, but perhaps the public won't dislike it. Anyhow, with Davidson at the helm and Watson at the prow, it will be a rare number.[64]

Harland is here referring to Davidson's poem, 'A Fleet Street Eclogue,' which appears last in the volume, and Watson's 'Hymn to the Sea,' which is the lead-off selection.

The omission of Beardsley, however, was indeed serious, for the art contents are decidedly uninteresting, except, perhaps, for a sketch of George Egerton and three drawings by Wilson Steer. The literary contents are also not distinguished. Harland's story, 'Rosemary for Remembrance,' concerned with a romance in Naples that leaves the narrator with faded memories, lacks the interest of some of his other stories. (Perhaps facetiously, he called it 'twaddle').[65] The major British periodicals did not review the volume, but in America, *The Bookman*, alluding to the Wilde trial without mentioning names, wrote of the new 'tone' of *The Yellow Book:* 'It is not only free from any suspicion of moral slime, but, in its literary features at least, appears to have abandoned its former eccentricity . . . and its principal stories are far more wholesome than most of those that Mr Harland has heretofore admitted to his paper.'[66]

In May, Harland's collection of short stories, *Grey Roses*, was published as Volume X of Lane's 'Keynotes Series,' the idea derived from George Egerton's *Keynotes*, with title pages by Beardsley, who continued to work for Lane after his dismissal from *The Yellow Book*. Consisting of five stories previously published in the first four volumes of *The Yellow Book* and four new stories, *Grey Roses* is the first of Harland's books in which the name of 'Sidney Luska' does not appear in parentheses on the title page. One of the new stories, in length a novelette, is entitled 'Castles Near Spain,' clearly a symbolic world of fantasy that Harland was later to re-create in his most successful novels, the sort of entertainment that Anthony Hope, in *The Prisoner of Zenda* (1894), became famous for. The tale, which takes place in 'Gascony, the borderland between amorous France and old romantic

Spain,' involves a young aristocrat's love for a beautiful, mysterious woman whom he sees daily riding through the forest. She is, it turns out, a queen, who, now living in quiet retirement, had, in fact, been a playmate of the young aristocrat during their childhood. Now separated from her husband, the king, re-marriage is, of course, out of the question, for she is a Catholic. Nevertheless, she and the aristocrat continue to meet, but for the sole purpose of indulging in a romance devoid of sensuality. Nothing of any significance occurs in the story, which is basically one of moods and symbolic poses. The static nature of art is alluded to by Harland in a letter to Le Gallienne earlier, in 1894, when, in referring to Flaubert's *L'Education sentimentale*, he writes : 'It is marvellous in that nothing ever happens – it is so like life.'[67] And one recalls Aline's letter to Stedman in 1893 in which she describes, in Jamesian terms, her husband's turning to a 'more sublimated' art, a 'less flesh and blood one.'

The association, at least, with James was not lost upon Harland's contemporaries. James is alluded to in Le Gallienne's review of *Grey Roses*, but clearly Harland is the master : 'In everything Mr Harland writes one feels the almost torturing fastidiousness of the artistic termperament in its most sensitive development ; yet not, as with his master, Mr Henry James, from any surface marks of strain upon his work.'[68] James and Harland are also associated in Frank Harris's attack on *Grey Roses* in the *Saturday Review:* 'Mr Harland, at times, almost conceals the feeble meaning of his stories by his studious avoidance of the obvious word. Mr Henry James, on the other hand, has eyes for human beings, and his singular distaste for the obvious is a thing to be regretted.'[69] Harland was later to respond to Harris's scathing reference to his 'conscientiously "original" mediocrity.'

In July, the sixth volume of *The Yellow Book* appeared,

the literary contents led by James's 'The Next Time.' Clearly, Harland had overcome James's aversion to the 'horrid aspect' of the periodical; it also signalled to the public that the enterprise was still very much alive. Another notable contribution was from the little known Arnold Bennett (then signing his work 'Enoch Arnold Bennett'), whose story, 'A Letter Home,' had been rejected elsewhere.[70] The volume also contains a number of essays, including the first of several 'Prose Fancies' by Le Gallienne. Harland's contribution, a story of memory, 'Tirala-tirala,' is one of his most Proustian pieces of writing involving the power of a tune to recapture the past. In this striking passage, which opens the story, Harland depicts the psychological process and the transcendent experience associated with the past:

> I wonder what the secret of it is – why that little fragment of a musical phrase has always had this instant, irresistible power to move me. The tune of which it formed a part I have never heard. . . . As when I was a child, so now, after all these years, it is a sort of talisman in my hands, a thing to conjure with. I have but to breathe it never so softly to myself, and (if I choose) the actual world melts away, and I am journeying on wings in dreamland. Whether I choose or not, it always thrills my heart with responsive echoes, it always wakes a sad, sweet emotion.

Reminiscent of Pater's 'The Child in the House,' Harland's story is about a house in which the memories of childhood haunt the mind of the narrator, the house merging as a symbol of a mysterious, lost innocence.

Harland, still in France, was corresponding with Lane on the financial problems of the April volume. The general mood of distrust resulting from the Wilde trial contributed to a considerable loss in sales. Writing on July 11, Harland informed Lane: 'On general principles I think I ought to be reimbursed for my actual out-of-pocket expenses in connection with the April *Y.B.*; but as you have lost so much on that number, I am content to lose a little.'[71] Their relationship, however, continued to be cordial, and Harland urged Lane to join him in Dieppe for part of his holiday : 'We'll bathe in the sea, and drink absinthe on the terrace of the casino, and lose our money at petits-chevaux, and do all sorts of amusing foolish things.'[72] In the meanwhile, Harland requested that manuscripts be sent to Cromwell Road, where his servant would wrap them into parcels for forwarding to Dieppe.[73]

Volume VII of *The Yellow Book* duly appeared in October with the same coterie of familiar names : Le Gallienne, Olive Custance, Ella D'Arcy, Hubert Crackanthorpe, Kenneth Grahame, and others. A notable new contributor was Frederick Rolfe ('Baron Corvo'), several of whose 'Stories Toto Told Me' appeared in the periodical. According to Donald Weeks, Rolfe, after several attempts to attract Harland's attention, wrote the first Toto stories in a public lavatory on paper usually found in such conveniences. Rolfe contended that only by this extraordinary method of submitting a manuscript did Harland at last show interest.[74] Harland became a good friend of Rolfe until there later occurred a falling out (characteristic of all of Rolfe's relationships), which, as we shall see, roused the 'Baron' to fury : he consequently ridiculed Harland, under various names, in several subsequent books.[75]

The seventh volume also contains the first appearance of a contribution from 'The Yellow Dwarf,' a new mask adopted by Harland to attack enemies (such as Frank Harris) and praise friends (such as those in *The Yellow Book* set). Designed as a long letter to the editor, the piece attempted to conceal its author's identity by including comments by Harland himself in footnotes that question or correct 'The Yellow Dwarf.' Harland may have wished to introduce the element of polemics into this issue in order to revitalize the quarterly, which had suffered in sales since the April issue. In his letter, 'The Yellow Dwarf' condemns such major periodicals as *The Athenaeum*, *The Academy*, *The Spectator*, and particularly Harris's *Saturday Review* for their inadequacies as critical journals. Harris, however, is the true object of Harland's attack because of the adverse review of *Grey Roses* and Harris's remark about Harland's 'conscientiously "original" mediocrity':

> I ransack the serried columns of the *Saturday Review* and its contemporaries and rivals, in vain, from week to week to discover my own thoughts and feelings about books accurately expressed in elegant and original sentences. . . . I discover plenty of pedantry and plenty of ignorance, plenty of feebleness and plenty of good stodgy 'ability,' plenty of glitter and plenty of dullness, plenty of fulsomeness and more than a plenty of envy, hatred, malice, and all uncharitableness ; but the thing I seek is the one thing I never find.[76]

Mrs Pearl Craigie and George Moore are also subjected to rather severe critical judgment. The Dwarf, for example, writes of Moore's style : 'It is a symmetrical temple built of soiled and broken bricks.' One wonders whether Harland was angered because Mrs Craigie and Moore never contributed more than the one act of their play to *The Yellow Book* (actually, they never completed it) and whether Harland still believed that Moore had written the abusive review of the first volume for *The Speaker*.

Though some readers may have been deceived by the Dwarf's identity, Harris was convinced that it was Harland : the Dwarf, he wrote, is 'as peevish, malicious and sickly as any dwarf of romance. He dislikes the *Saturday Review* and its present editor, and he has particular good reason to dislike them. Did not the *Saturday Review* poke fun at "Grey Roses"? The "Yellow Dwarf" is Mr Henry Harland. The jargon he writes, a sort of Frenchified English that shows ignorance of both languages, is as characteristic of him as the parti-coloured hose was of Malvolio. We had had Mr Harland's praise in the past over his signature; we now have his blame from behind a mask; we prefer the blame, and Mr Harland need not conceal his identity.'[77] But Harland and Lane pretended that Harris was wrong, perhaps to provoke him further and thereby stimulate more publicity. In the following week, Lane placed an advertisement in the *Saturday Review*, which reads in part: 'The editor of the *Saturday* asserts boldly that the *Yellow Dwarf* is Mr Henry Harland. But that, after all, is only one of the thousand guesses everybody is making.'[78] The rest of the advertisement gives quotes from other periodicals as to who the Yellow Dwarf might be, *The Queen* believing, for example, that it is an 'unsnubbable school-boy.' In his 'London Letter' to *The Critic*, Arthur Waugh, referring to the 'ill-mannered article' by the 'Yellow Dwarf,' mentions the advertisement, 'full of gibes,' in the *Saturday Review* and concludes that 'it is very vulgar.'[79]

Harland's story in the seventh volume, 'The Queen's Pleasure,' combines, in a rather odd manner, images of the Latin Quarter with a setting in an imaginary kingdom. The narrator had known a youth, in his student days in Paris, who is now the king of a 'Danubian principality' with a German wife. Lengthy and slow in its development, the story depicts the queen's sudden ousting of the prime minister, later found to have made a 'secret treaty' with Berlin. The queen, distressed by her subjects' hatred of her despite the truth about the prime minister, laments: 'Oh, the folly of universal suffrage! The folly of constitutional government! I used to say, "Surely a good despot is better than a mob." But now I'm convinced that a *bad* despot, even, is better.' The 'shop-keeping class' alone speak up for her because she spends money freely, but 'they are aliens and don't count – or, rather, they count against her, "the dogs of Jews"...' The story is poor but significant, for it reveals a curious portrayal of the faceless, unrepresented 'mob' that the queen scorns and, as we have seen before, an increasing interest, in Harland's fiction, in idyllic, at times pastoral, versions of nobility. At the same time, anti-Semitism, later more prominent, makes its first appearance here. Interestingly, it was at this time that Harland attempted to trace his family to the Harlands of Suffolk, England, in order to establish a claim to a baronetcy.[80]

Returning to London from Paris in the autumn, Harland faced a formidable rival that would seriously challenge the future of *The Yellow Book*: this new periodical was *The Savoy*, edited by Arthur Symons and Beardsley, the first issue of which was to appear in January, 1896. In November, Waugh, in his 'London Letter' to *The Critic*, wrote : 'If *The Savoy* is half as good as it promises to be, it will knock the reputation out of the *Yellow Book* in one number.'[81] Unlike Harland, Symons and his co-editor would not have to contend with a publisher who was ready to impose restraints on the nature of the contents, for Leonard Smithers, the publisher of *The Savoy*, had a taste for the arcane and pornographic in literature and sought out Symons because he was the acknowledged spokesman for Decadence in literature.[82] The first issue (and subsequent issues) revealed that Symons, in his ability to obtain work from the leading Symbolists and Decadents of both France and Britain, was a brilliant editor who made *The Savoy* the first truly British avant-garde publication of the 1890s. In addition, Beardsley's illustrations and prose tale, 'Under the Hill,' revealed a new source of creative brilliance only hinted at in *The Yellow Book*. No doubt, Lane and Harland were worried when the first issue of *The Savoy* appeared.

In January, 1896, both *The Savoy* and the eighth

volume of *The Yellow Book* appeared, the latter consisting of 406 pages, the weightiest volume yet, possibly an attempt by Harland to outweigh the new rival. Two new important contributors that Harland secured were George Gissing ('The Foolish Virgin') and H. G. Wells ('A Slip under the Microscope'), their only appearance in *The Yellow Book*. Most of the other contributors were familiar to the faithful. Harland's story, 'P'tit Bleu,' depicts the life of a whore who abandons her gay Bohemian world to devote herself to an English painter addicted to drugs (another version of the failed artist). Why she undertakes her new life is never made clear, but the element of self-sacrifice reveals Harland's moral, even Puritanical, attitude.

Also included in this volume is Olive Custance's poem, 'A Mood,' which stimulated a correspondence between the poet and Harland quite unlike the usual exchange of letters between a contributor and an editor. As yet, Harland, who had been publishing Custance's poems in preceding volumes, had not met her, and we may presume that his previous letters were primarily concerned with the business of the periodical. However, as Custance noted in her diary on January 4, 1896, Harland responded to the flattery in one of her letters: 'H. Harland – clever Editor of the *Y.B.* – wrote me a most charming letter the other day – and only because I sent "A Mood" – corrected – direct to him and told him truely [*sic*] how much I liked some of his work.'[83]

A series of eight letters that has survived[84] reveal Harland in an unusual state of mind, for they are love letters to this young girl of twenty-two (Harland was thirty-four). Yet, they are also strangely anti-romantic: Harland continually speaks of his age as though life and love were over for him. Though part of his attitude was probably a pose, he was either reluctant or fearful to pursue his epistolary romance beyond the pillar-box and enjoyed the innocent fantasy of a chaste flirtation, as he apparently enjoyed writing of such romances in his fiction. So far as is known, Harland was always faithful to Aline, who shared his public life as intimately as his private life (as we have seen, she wrote in the first person plural – the editorial 'we' – when describing the success of *The Yellow Book*). Ella D'Arcy has stated, 'You could not think of the Harlands separately. They were always together.'[85] Yet, they were regarded, by contemporary accounts, as an 'erratic' couple. One may conclude that their marriage was a stormy, albeit a close one.

One of the roles that Harland assumed in his letters to Olive Custance was that of confessor and comforter. In a letter probably written early in January, 1896, he attempts to dissipate her pessimism, which emerges with some frequency in her letters to him :

> You mustn't say that you expect nothing from life. You are standing at the gateway of the Castle of Enchantment, and you say, 'I expect nothing from the labyrinthian galleries, and shining halls, the courts, the treasure-chambers, that are waiting for me, their Chatelaine.' On the contrary, you must expect everything. And believe me, you'll get what you expect, what you demand. Gold, or lead, or ashes, you'll get what you demand. It's those who don't expect, who don't demand anything, that get nothing.

Commenting on a new poem, 'Sunshine,' that she had sent to him for the April issue, Harland writes : 'I think this new poem, in its way, one of the most exquisite you have done ; it is so musical, so imaginative, and so finely emotional. I know comparisons are odious, but shall I tell you that of all the poetry we have published in the *Yellow Book*, it is yours which moves me most, which seems to me most poetical?' Again turning to her pessimism, he writes in the same letter : 'But *why*, *why* do you fall into such pessimistic moods, and say that you expect nothing from life, and that it is best to be silent? Silent? But "mere clay clods" can be silent. It is your duty to sing – to live and to sing. Ah, si jeunesse savait !'

He had the Bodley Head send a copy of the January volume of *The Yellow Book* to her ; she responded with praise for his story, 'P'tit Bleu,' and requested a photograph of him :

> My photograph? I have not had a photograph taken since 1882 – only think, fourteen years ! And you were in the Nursery then. And I was twenty, and in Rome. . . ah, me ! But if I ever should have another taken, be sure I will send it to you. What am I like? Oh, quite like everybody : the usual height, the usual age, the usual complexion. But you. . .! I have seen a photograph of Miss Custance at the Bodley Head. I do devoutly wish she would send me a duplicate of it. Do, *please*.

He urges her to write to him again so that she might tell him 'lots more' than she had told him before :

> A beautiful letter, a beautiful white *Song-Bird*, from the girl, the beautiful poet-girl, who signs herself my little friend ! My little friend – with the wonderful burning soul, the deep burning heart, the great yearning eyes, looking out upon the Norfolk landscape, away, away, towards the horizon where she divines the world, look-ing, and wondering, and longing. Oh, sometimes it seems as if her heart must break with that desperate, unsatisfied longing – as if her soul could not endure such hunger any more. I know, I know. I know how she hungers, how she suffers. Why can I do nothing for her? All I can do is to bid her be of good courage, trust her Star. Yes, the same Star that made you a Poet will see to it that you shall have a Poet's life, a full life. But it is hard to wait.

In another letter, Harland describes his disappointment when, upon awakening, there is no letter from her ; however, while dressing, he hears a knock at his door ; it is the postman, who has brought him a parcel from her :

> And then, of course, I just wondered and wondered

what it could contain. Do you think my fingers trembled as I opened it?

Oh, what can I say, what can I say? The exquisite white flowers, like little white spirits, and the exquisite violets ! And to think that *you* picked them, you, you, – for me ! It is too delicious. And their scent – their delicious, penetrating, sweet scent . . . what *is* it it whispers? Something beautiful, something thrilling-sweet, I know ; but in a language my old wayworn heart is not pure enough to understand. I can only dimly guess at the translation – but the beauty and the thrilling sweetness I can acutely feel, even if I can't understand it.

The letter proceeds to the edge of a personal confession :

There is nothing I can say. Or, if I *should* say what I want to say, what I long to say . . . oh, but I mustn't. – Why do you imply that I don't mean what I say? You know that the fact is just the contrary – I don't say more than a hundredth part of what I mean – of what I should like to say. But the little I do say I mean with all my heart – though I am a 'naughty tease.'

Indeed, a 'naughty tease' who speaks from behind the mask of feigned old age and thus protects himself from temptation. In this same letter, he assures her that his age is far more advanced than hers : 'You have overtaken me – you hail me as you pass.' Harland is perhaps borrowing from Max Beerbohm's essay, 'Be It Cosiness,' which had appeared in the December, 1895, issue of *The Pageant*, where, with feigned weariness, Max strikes the dandiacal pose: 'Already I feel myself a trifle outmoded. I belong to the Beardsley period. Younger men, with months of activity before them, with fresher schemes and notions, with newer enthusiasm, have pressed forward since then.' Max was twenty-three. In his letter to Olive Custance, Harland, striking similar poses, refers to himself as a 'wayworn tired old sinner' and uses the third person pronoun in a rather depersonalized way, again uncharacteristic of the romantic lover : 'His heart is moved to say a thousand things to you – to catch you by the hand and implore you for mercy's sake *not* to pass on. . . .' The innuendoes continue in the letter, as they do in others : '. . . he doesn't need to say it. You know it. You can hear it in the vibrations of his voice. And, besides. . . . And, besides. . . . And, besides. . . .'

When she promised to send him her photograph, Harland, in another letter, thanked her for the forthcoming 'adorable photograph' : 'But think how impatient I shall be now, until it comes. Do make the photographer hurry up. Oh, it was good of you, sweet of you, to have it taken for me.' Apparently, she posed for the photograph with Harland's letter in her hand – at least, that seems to be the implication in the following : 'And my poor letter – it must have blushed red, for joy, for pride. If it did, it will come out (as red things do) *black*, in the picture. If it didn't it's an ungrateful monster of a letter, and deserves to be drawn, quartered, and burned at the stake. As for me, *my* joy, *my* pride, are quite inexpressible. Why can't I *see* you, and try to let you know?'

Having been asked by her to describe himself, Harland obliges in his customary manner by inventing fantasies of his youth ; first, however, he must lend credibility to his tale by giving a truthful picture of his physical appearance :

> Alas, there is so little to describe. A middle-aged young man seated at a table, writing ; rather tall (five feet eleven), very thin, with a dark skin, dark hair rapidly turning grey (almost *white* on top), and grey eyes with an unmistakable snub-nose between them. For the rest, a short pointed beard, rather prominent cheek-bones, and a pince-nez. . . . Now aren't you disillusioned? . . . Not at all an English face – a *Slav* type of face. . . . A middle-aged young man whose life, from the day he was born, until, at last, a few years ago, he settled down in London, was one perpetual *move* from town to town, country to country. He was born in St. Petersburg,

and passed most of his childhood in Rome, old *papal* Rome, and most of his youth in France, and two or three years of his early manhood in America (worse luck), and now is a Literary Hack in London, sorry termination. Therefore, rather a cynical, suspicious, disenchanted person, and horribly frivolous, ribald, almost never serious. Oh, I don't believe you would like him.

Looking forward to seeing her in March, he rhapsodizes:

Yes, yes, yes, it is *Wild Olive* whom I must meet when you come to town – in March, far-away March. *Where* shall we meet? *How* shall we meet? I shall burn a perpetual taper to the Saints who arrange such meetings, till ours has come to pass. It is really very wonderful that we should meet at all. Starting from such different points in space, in time, and following such different pathways – isn't it strange that in this perilous wilderness of a world we should ever have found each other? And if you knew all the circumstances, it would seem stranger still.

Is Harland alluding, in his mysterious manner, to his unromantic past (his Brooklyn birth, his years at City College in New York, his clerkship in the Surrogate's office) and to his marriage, subjects that would obviously shatter his epistolary romance? After having concluded this letter with questions about a book of poems that she was preparing for publication, he adds a sudden postscript:

Oh, that sweet, sweet word at the very top of the first page of that sweetest letter. 'That YOU may tell me I am young!' That was thrilling sweet – dear friend.

I am writing 'Cousin Rosalys' *to* you. I hope I have your permission. Do please (in spirit) look over my shoulder as I write, and teach me how to make it worthy of you – my . . . little friend.

Harland's story, 'Cousin Rosalys,' is a sentimental tale of lost love, a narrator recalling his romance, at the age of eighteen, with a 'cousin' when he visits his great-aunt in Rome. Once again, the setting is pastoral, with a great Roman 'palace' and beside the terrace a beautiful old Roman garden, 'a fragrant, romantic garden,' complete with statues of pagan gods and goddesses. The narrator, on looking back, recalls his romantic attraction to his cousin : 'If at eighteen one isn't susceptible and sentimental and impetuous, and prepared to respond with an instant sweet commotion to the smiles of one's pretty cousin (especially when they're named Rosalys), I protest one is unworthy of one's youth. One might as well be thirty-five, and a literary hack in London.' The allusion to himself (Harland was thirty-five when the story appeared in the April, 1896, volume of *The Yellow Book* and the phrase 'literary hack' was facetiously used in his letter to Custance) was employed, no doubt, for the amusement of his 'dear friend.' In the story, the narrator tells of his 'double life' : his carefree existence among Bohemian artists and his proper, correct behaviour when he visits his aunt (is this a reflection of Harland's 'double life' as well?). Rosalys is remarkably like Olive Custance, and possibly Harland modelled his character after the photograph that he had seen at the Bodley Head : 'Her delicate, pale face, and her dark, undulating hair, and her soft red lips ; and then her eyes, – her luminous, mysterious dark eyes, in whose depths, far, far within, you could discern her spirit shining starlike.' And as the narrator proceeds to describe their relationship, he sounds very much like Harland himself in his inability – or reluctance – to express his love : '. . . I loved her so ! Oh, why couldn't I tell her? Why couldn't she divine it? People said that women always knew by intuition when men were in love with them. Why couldn't Rosalys divine that I loved her, *how* I loved her, and make me a sign, and so enable me to speak?'

After confessing his love for her, the narrator asks his aunt to sanction their engagement. For this, he is driven from the house : 'Adam and Eve were driven from Eden for their guilt ; but it was Innocence that lost our Eden for Rosalys and me.' He is called home ; some years later, Rosalys marries the nephew of a Cardinal and later dies. Harland may have written his story as an allegory expressing his innocent love of Olive Custance, aware that such relationships inevitably die. To express it in the guise of fiction, with such romantic trappings as the symbolic garden and palace, and to linger upon the innocence of the lovers and the death of the young girl suggest the self-indulgence of the sentimentalist.

In another letter, Harland responds to Custance's query concerning his 'favourite poets.' He prefers, he writes, French poetry to English poetry :

> To me, French as a language is so much more poetical than good, practical, serviceable, commercial English. French is fragrant with sentiment, hot with passion. But amongst English poets – don't you care for Browning? Oh, yes, and Rossetti. But I think I read Browning more frequently than any other poet. Perhaps that's because I'm OLD, and have lost most of my illusions. When I was young I worshipped Swinburne. For Shelley my love has never gone beyond the Platonic.

But this letter is also passionate in its address, especially when he denies that he could ever tire of her letters : '. . . your beautiful, beautiful, beautiful letters, every syllable of which I read a hundred times? Letters so worn with life, so fragrant of the girl who writes them . . . *I* have certainly never received such letters, such lovely letters.' And in another letter, the same note is struck : 'I thought I had felt everything, experienced the whole gamut of possible human emotion. I thought my capacity for emotion was exhausted. And now. . . . ! I have listened to the singing of a Soul, and I have learned that there is a new joy, a new pain. . . . You force me to revise my conclusions about life, to throw overboard a whole cargo of beliefs.' He has discovered, he tells her, 'at least one woman

6. Harland in 1903
[From *The Lamp* (New York), 26 n.s. (April, 1903), 227.]

7. Harland's Grave at Yantic Cemetery, Norwich Town, Conn.
[Photograph by Karl Beckson.]

ALINE M. HARLAND

DIED AUG. 27, 1939.

8. Aline Harland's Grave at Yantic Cemetery, Norwich Town, Conn.
[Photograph by Karl Beckson.]

9. Ella D'Arcy (in the 1890s)
[From the E. C. Stedman Papers, Columbia University.]

10. E. C. Stedman (in 1892, aged 59)
[From the E. C. Stedman Papers, Columbia University.]

in the world radically and essentially different to [*sic*] all others : one strong, passionate, original, authentic woman : individual, unique. Thank Heaven I have met her before it is too late.'

His discovery is all the more significant, because in England, people conceal their passions under 'starch and whalebone and conventions,' he tells her in another letter :

> In France, where my home is, it is different. But in England people are ashamed of their humanity. It is an Englishman's second nature to endeavour to smother, suffocate, annihilate his first. They suppress all expression of emotion, till the emotions themselves atrophy and die – but you ! You are real. You suffer, you enjoy, you hope and fear and desire and love and hate ; you are alive ; there is blood in your veins, and the blood is hot and scarlet and palpitant: and your reality, so far from being ashamed of itself or trying to conceal or stifle itself, sings itself in beautiful poems, in beautiful letters.

In this letter, he again urges her to abandon her pessimism about life, for she is 'only at the threshold' : 'Mercy ! how I envy you – young, and beautiful, and a poet ! How I envy you the good years that are waiting for you, the unspoilt years. Oh, you will see that I am right.'

She finally sent him her photograph after a lapse of some time. Harland, responding to her letter, despaired of ever having heard from her : 'I thought you were tired of me, and tired of my letters, – as you well might be ; and I was in the *deeps*, the deepest deeps, of sorrow and anger.' The photograph is that of the 'loveliest girl, the most interesting-looking, the most poetic-looking, the most appealing, that I have ever seen.' Her 'dreamy, mysterious eyes' recall Rosalys' in Harland's story, and he tells her that he yearns to look into the 'real eyes.' He mentions that she has said that in March she was coming to London : presumably they would meet then. The letter closes: 'You know ALL I DO NOT SAY.'

In what circumstances Harland and Custance finally met is unknown; however, she visited the Harlands at their Cromwell Road flat on Saturday nights. More than one writer recalls her presence there.

In April, 1896, the ninth volume of *The Yellow Book* appeared with another contribution from 'The Yellow Dwarf,' this time 'A Birthday Letter' commemorating the second anniversary of the publication of the quarterly. Harland again attacks Frank Harris and attempts to keep speculation fresh by denying that the Dwarf is either Max Beerbohm, Saintsbury, Rider Haggard, Mrs Humphry Ward, or Henry Harland. Raising the question of the *Saturday Review*'s hostility towards the editor of *The Yellow Book*, the Dwarf enquires whether the editor of *The Yellow Book* has ever rejected a manuscript submitted by a member of the *Saturday Review* staff. The Dwarf welcomes the appointment of Alfred Austin as Poet Laureate, though he refers to him as 'Pressman Laureate.' Much of the letter, however, is devoted to an attack on George du Maurier's popular novel, *Trilby*. Other contributors to the volume are Max Beerbohm ('Poor Romeo'), Frederick Rolfe (two more 'Stories Toto Told Me'), Richard Le Gallienne ('Four Prose Fancies'), Olive Custance ('Sunshine'), and John Buchan ('A Journey of Little Profit'). The volume is not distinguished, in either its literary or art contents; the press declined to review it.

In July, the tenth volume appeared, but there is no notable improvement upon the previous issue. Most curious is Harland's 'Yellow Dwarf' contribution, 'Dogs, Cats, Books, and the Common Man,' a *tour de force* that expresses an anti-democratic point of view associated with the Aesthetic Movement. Asserting that the Average Man loves the Dog (an 'all-pervading plebeian commonness hangs about him') rather than the Cat (a 'Princess' with 'high-bred reserve and dignity'), Harland proceeds to characterize the Average Man himself as 'gross mutton-devouring, money-grubbing mech-anism that he is.' The Dwarf's letter is also an indication of how the 'worship' of Art in the late nineteenth century, associated with the idea that only an intellectual élite could comprehend such art, moved progressively to the right in politics and religion, influencing such later figures as Yeats, Wyndham Lewis, T. S. Eliot, Lawrence, and Pound.

In his essay, Harland regards vulgar, common books as 'the very Dogs of Bookland,' and those books that are 'deli-cate, distinguished, aristocratic' are the 'Cats of Bookland,' which the Average Man 'hates' or 'ignores.' Harland names Dog and Cat books, and, as one might expect, refers to the work of such *Yellow Book* writers as Ella D'Arcy, Hubert Crackanthorpe, and Kenneth Grahame as 'Cat-Literature.' Indeed, the 'Yellow Dwarf' even refers to 'Mr Harland [who] has given us some very pretty Grey Kittens,' and, to be sure, 'in any proper Cat Show, the Cats of Mr Henry James would carry off the special grand *prix d'honneur*.' As one can see, the essay is decidedly heavy handed.

Harland's story for this volume, 'The Invisible Prince,' depicts, once again, an imaginary kingdom in which the prince adopts the mask of a poet (indeed, the story opens with a masked ball), in order to escape from the obligations of his position (as though, in some way, art involves no responsi-bilities). He has a romance that includes much witty dialogue but little else (much like Harland's romance with Olive Custance). There is also a tirade by the prince against the 'People,' consistent with Harland's own intolerance of the Average Man as expressed in his 'Yellow Dwarf' letter.

The issue of masks arose in the October volume when Harland included Beerbohm's drawing of 'The Yellow Dwarf,' depicting an elfish, rotund figure wearing a fringed mask and holding a bow and arrow. A writer in *The Critic* was convinced that

... Mr Harland stands confessed by the caricature. I reproduce herewith Mr Beerbohm's gentle compliment to his friend, and also an amateur photograph of Mr Harland, and I leave it to the reader to say whether or not they are the same. Note the turn of the eye in the caricature : is it not the same as in the photograph? Note, also, the pointed beard in each and the tilt of the nose. Tear off the mask, and you have the face of Henry Harland— or put the mask on the face of Henry Harland, and you have the Yellow Dwarf. The figures, I admit, are not the same. There Mr Harland has the advantage.[86]

The Beerbohm caricature has a slight connection with the character of a cupid dwarf in his tale, 'The Happy Hypocrite,' that leads off the eleventh volume. Indeed, the literary contents of the volume seem decidedly improved with Beerbohm's contribution as well as Reggie Turner's 'A Chef-d'oeuvre,' concerned with the failed artist, one of Harland's prominent themes. Harland's story, 'The Friend of Man,' is a notably superior effort, concerned with the personality of a social philosopher named Ambrose, who seems to have been modelled after Harland's step-grand-father, Stephen Pearl Andrews. In the story, the narrator states, '... during the great part of my childhood, Augustus Ambrose lived with us, was virtually a member of our family,' as, in fact, Andrews did with the Harlands. Ambrose, like Andrews, invents a universal language and writes enormous tomes embracing massive themes, such as Andrews' 'Universology.' Yet, Ambrose lacks any genuine affection for the common man. The story is interesting with respect to Harland himself, for, in his youth, he was reared in a liberal, egalitarian setting. Is he here tracing, in symbolic form, the movement of his own mind? Is he dramatizing a disturbing problem of his own?

In January, 1897, the twelfth volume of *The Yellow*

Book appeared with a number of the same writers who had appeared in its inaugural volume: James, Le Gallienne, Grahame, D'Arcy, Watson, Garnett, and others who had appeared in several succeeding volumes. *The Savoy* had already expired with the December, 1896, issue, partly the result of W. H. Smith & Son's refusal to handle copies in their news-stands because of an illustration by Blake, and partly because Smithers underestimated expenses of production and overestimated sales when he made the quarterly a monthly with the August issue. But Symons principally blamed the public for not supporting an artistic publication: '... worst of all, we assumed that there were very many people in the world who really cared for art, and really for art's sake.'[87] If *The Savoy* ended, despite its superior literary and artistic contents, it was only a matter of time before *The Yellow Book*, which appealed to a somewhat similar audience, would follow suit. To some extent, it had been able to survive precisely because it had remained a quarterly, but its next issue, Volume XIII, to appear in April, would be its last, exactly three years after its first appearance.

The art of Volume XII reached a new low: *The Times* could only notice its existence but say little with any enthusiasm, and of its literary contents, the review stated: 'The principle upon which the *Yellow Book* is edited would seem to be that at intervals of every three months a section of the reading public is seized with a craving for fresh work by Mr Henry Harland, Miss Ella D'Arcy, and others of the little school of writers whom the Bodley Head has brought into notice.'[88] The review points to what was apparently Harland's error: the retention of the same coterie of writers, most of them minor; and if Lane wished to retain the group because he was also publishing their books (hoping, perhaps, to extract profit from such reinforcement of public exposure), then he too contributed to the death of the periodical.

Harland's contribution to this volume, 'Flower o' the Clove,' is of some interest if only for its seeming autobiographical elements, for it involves a writer who has some claim to nobility but is insensitive in matters of romance. Harland's 'Yellow Dwarf' does not appear in this volume, nor in the final volume: if Harland had attempted to stir controversy with his vitriolic mask, he succeeded only in writing himself out of existence.

The death of *The Yellow Book* had been foreshadowed as early as July, 1896, when Harry Thurston Peck wrote in the American *Bookman*: 'We understand that Messrs. Copeland and Day [American publishers] will discontinue the publication of *The Yellow Book*. The literature of this quarterly is better now than ever, yet since Aubrey Beardsley dropped out of it, its popular vogue seems to have declined.'[89] Harland included no editorial note on the demise of the quarterly, as Symons had done in the final issue of *The Savoy*. Possibly, he did not know at the time of its publication that it would not appear again.

The volume opens with Yeats's Celtic poem, 'The Blessed,' his only appearance in *The Yellow Book*; in addition, there are the usual contributors seen before. Interestingly, there are three prose pieces concerned with sensational deaths: 'A Pair of Parricides' by Francis Watt, gives a gruesome account of two actual murder cases; Cecil de Thierry's 'On the Toss of a Penny' is a short story involving terror and death; and Ella D'Arcy's 'Sir Julian Garve' is about a gambler who comes to a bad end. Harland's story, however, titled 'Merely Players,' exists in a different world: it involves a retreat from sordidness and death. Its central figure, a gentleman who lives in a castle, has a romance, at once idyllic and pastoral, with a tall beautiful girl who strolls periodically through a garden near the castle. As any reader of Harland might expect, the gentleman is the monarch of the country and the beautiful girl is the queen whom he has married by proxy but whom he has never seen. The end is inevitable. Seemingly aware of the nature of his own art, Harland concludes the story abruptly : 'And then — but I think I have told enough.'

Aline Harland has written that her husband's poor health 'was the cause of the *Yellow Book's* end.'[90] This reason may, however, be only one of a number why the periodical died. As we have seen, the dependence on a coterie of minor writers may have been a major factor, and Lane's failure or unwillingness to pay major artists to contribute may have been another. Ella D'Arcy, no doubt with some facetiousness, accounted for its end : 'We were all a little tired of it.'[91] Later a director of the Bodley Head put it in a more business-like manner : 'It had ceased to pay dividends.'[92]

Whatever the reasons, the brief life of *The Yellow Book* enabled Harland to propel himself to the centre of the English literary world, despite hostility from some quarters. It also provided him with an immediate source of publication, both as a writer of short stories and as a critic.[93] Whereas he had complained, when writing stories for McClure's syndicate in the 1880s, that newspapers had mangled his texts and changed his titles, he had the complete freedom, rare for any writer, to publish exactly what he wished in his own quarterly. But beyond these personal advantages, Harland, as an editor, revealed an intense devotion to an artistic level of imaginative expression, and if he could not always attract the greatest writers of the age to contribute to the quarterly, he attempted to include the best available without compromise. Beerbohm regarded him as an excellent editor, and in his fictional memoir of the period, 'Enoch Soames,' he refers to Harland as 'the most joyous of men and most generous of critics' ;[94] another contributor to *The Yellow Book* wrote that 'the number of those whom [Harland] helped, whom he toiled for and encouraged is amazing.'[95]

With the publication of the final volume in April, 1897, Harland, at the age of thirty-six, in desperate financial circumstances, his position of power and prestige now gone, faced an uncertain future. Yet, the passing of momentary glory did not end his literary career, for, in the years to come, he attained notoriety and wealth that far exceeded the successes of the 'Sidney Luska' years.

CHAPTER FIVE

The Last Years (1897-1905)

═══════════════════════════════════

URING THE FINAL month of his duties as editor of
The Yellow Book, Harland repeatedly asked Lane for
payment of editorial work completed. 'I'm stony-
broke,' he wrote in one letter,[1] an indication that he could not
devote time to writing for the more lucrative periodicals.
Now free, he accepted an invitation to review Owen Seaman's
The Battle of the Bays for *The Academy* (though some of Seaman's parodies ridiculed *Yellow Book* writers, Harland called
them 'incomparably delightful').[2] He also wrote an essay
on the short story,[3] important for an understanding of his
aesthetics, that reveals the depth of his admiration for James
and indeed may have resulted in the Master's reciprocal
appreciation of Harland's *Comedies and Errors* in the following
year.

In his article on the short story, Harland makes a
distinction between what a writer does with an 'impression'
once he has it and what the 'normal man' does with it, for a
story, he states, does not begin with an 'idea' or an 'incident'
but with an 'impression' : '. . . if you are a normal man, you
are content with having got your impression – you stop there :
while if you are an artist you are constantly possessed by a
desire to give your impressions expression in the particular
form of art it is your joy and your despair to cultivate.' A short
story is not measurable by the number of pages : '. . . that
story is a short story . . . in which you have expressed your

impression with the greatest economy of means.' Like Pater and Symons, who both stressed the essential nature of experience in terms of fleeting impressions that undergo artistic transformation into the symbolic 'moments' of a work of art, Harland suggests that an impression must be analyzed and studied before writing may proceed, until the impression is purified by the writer :

> His difficulty will be, by selecting the essential, the significant, by rigidly excluding the unessential, by trusting as much as ever he may to the experience and imagination of his reader, and, finally, and chiefly, by bestowing unstinted pains upon his manner of writing, so that each phrase, each word, each comma, shall be indispensable and right and effective – his difficulty will be to present his impression in the briefest space in which it can be presented without losing any of its significance or any of its beauty.

Harland extols James as 'the supreme prince of short story writers' who surpasses Maupassant. Designed to be read with care, James's stories are not for the unenlightened, Harland insists, or for those who read in commuter trains, for James's impressions are complex. With respect to 'achieving the requisite brevity,' Harland states that James does this in two ways : 'One way is to throw his story into perspective, to remove it a certain distance back in point of time ; then to tell it as one speaking from memory, who sees his vision through a softening medium, which blurs what is trivial and unmeaning, but heightens all that is salient and suggestive.' Harland attempted such a technique in a number of his own stories, particularly his Proustian ones, and his appreciation of James's genius and success reveals the extent of his own failure, for Harland's fatal attraction to romantic sentimentality diminished any strength he may have learned from James. Harland was acutely, even painfully, aware of his inferiority to the Master. In 1903, he remarked to an interviewer, who had said that the two writers had been put on the same level of creative ability : 'I? Oh, what am I, what can I ever do that I should exist in the same sentence with Henry James? A mere butterfly perched above a boulder – a mote, a speck dancing in the great, full beam!'[4]

In November, 1897, Aline left hurriedly for America to be at the bedside of her ailing mother, who died on November 17. She remained for six weeks to be with her father. While in New York, Aline visited Stedman, who wrote to a friend on November 21 : '. . . the paragon of lovely and clever womanhood is here to-day, my old time pet Mrs Henry Harland — on a flying trip to America for the first time in seven years. She is not a day older in looks, nor a bit spoiled by crowded experiences, but with some wondrous added perfection of voice, motion, look, which the years have given her.'[5] During Aline's stay in America, Harland spent Christmas in Paris, but on his return, as he wrote to Gosse, he had apparently 'caught a chill' on the train and was forced to remain in bed 'with a sufficiently tiresome combination of bronchitis and laryngitis.'[6]

In late 1897, Harland had arranged with Lane to publish a collection of short stories, most of which had already appeared in Volumes V to XIII of *The Yellow Book*. Published in March, 1898, as *Comedies and Errors*, 'a ripping old title,' as Harland referred to it,[7] the volume contains three new stories. If, as Albert Parry has suggested, James believed that 'he must reciprocate in kind, however reservedly,'[8] for Harland's high praise in his article on the short story, his review of *Comedies and Errors* is rather diffuse, indirect criticism that may, as Parry states, be designed 'to mask its forced character.' The review is acute, however, in its perception of Harland's vision of Europe : 'He is lost in the vision, all whimsical and picturesque, of palace secrets, rulers and pretenders and ministers of bewilderingly light comedy, in undiscoverable

Balkan states, Bohemias of the seaboard, where the queens have platonic relationships with professional English, though not American, humorists; in the heavy, many-voiced air of the old Roman streets and of the high Roman salons where cardinals are part of the furniture. . .' Harland, says James, had 'a form so compact and an execution so light and firm,' but, he concludes, '[Harland] is just yet, I think, a little too much everywhere, a trifle astray, as regards his inspiration, in the very wealth of his memories and the excess, even, of his wit.'[9] Only one or two stories are mentioned for special praise in what James calls 'the collection of curiously ingenious prose pieces'; the qualifications, however are obvious. Despite the rather curious review, it was evidently believed that James had publicly approved of Harland, for when the younger novelist died seven years later, *The Times* stated that with the publication of *Comedies and Errors* 'the delicate beauty of his writing was now acknowledged by the chief living authorities, and particularly by so refined a judge as Mr Henry James.'[10]

Pleased by James's review, Harland wrote to Gosse: 'Have you seen James's adorable article in the *Fortnightly*?',[11] In November of that year, Harland contributed an article, 'Mr Henry James,' to *The Academy* that goes beyond his earlier praise in 'Concerning the Short Story.' Indeed, Harland's article signals the beginning of cult worship, for it contends that James undertakes the impossible but always achieves it. The Master, clearly, can do no wrong: 'An intenser, finer insight, served by a technique nearer to perfection, a freer, firmer, more accomplished hand, and guided, restrained, by a more exacting, a more sensitive literary conscience – that is the word one first feels impelled to speak, when asked to speak a word about Mr Henry James.'[12] Leon Edel has written that James 'glowed' in Harland's praise.[13]

Some time in 1898, the Harlands were both received

into the Roman Catholic Church, thus following many associated with the Aesthetic Movement, such as Lionel Johnson, Ernest Dowson, John Gray, and Aubrey Beardsley, who sought certainty in faith and beauty in ritual. At the end of the nineteenth century, when, for many, art itself had become a religion, it was only a further step for religion to become the supreme art. Harland, according to Aline, had early in his life been attracted to Catholicism. After he had settled in London, his stories were often set in Rome frequently with churchmen as characters ; and his progressive pre-occupation with royalty in his tales also suggests a growing conservatism. Writing of their conversion, Aline states :

> One had not rather try even to narrate the facts which preceded this fortunate event, except to say that Henry Harland had, in spirit, been of the True Faith for many years. He was what is called an 'intellectually convinced Catholic.' He had the metaphysical mind. Their [i.e., the Harlands'] instruction by Father Charnley, S.J., did not draw out points of argument or of difficulty on Henry Harland's side, because, evidently, he was already enlightened and convinced regarding the dogma of Holy Mother Church.[14]

Beardsley's illness and conversion in 1897 may have been an influence in Harland's decision to join the Church. What impressed Harland was Beardsley's sincerity in his own conversion. In writing his friend's obituary in 1898, Harland stated : 'He became beautifully, serenely devout – not in any morbid or effeminate sense, but in the right sense, the wholesome, manly sense. His heart, his life, were filled with the joy and the love it is the merit of the Supreme Faith to bestow. In all his wretched bodily suffering . . . he had that to help him.'[15] Harland, who had also known what suffering was, sought an answer to the mystery of its existence.

In February, 1899, a curious visitor appeared at 144 Cromwell Road, wearing soiled, frayed clothing and an unkempt beard. It was Frederick Rolfe ('Baron Corvo'), who had just been to see Lane at the Bodley Head about his second volume of *Stories Toto Told Me* (the first volume had appeared in September, 1898) and about possible employment with the publisher, whom he later described in his novel *Nicholas Crabbe* (1958) as a 'tubby little pot-bellied bantam, scrupulously attired and looking as though he had been suckled on bad beer.' Noncommittal with respect to the book and unable to offer employment, Lane suggested that he see Harland, whom Rolfe had never met but with whom he had corresponded. That first meeting is dramatized in *Nicholas Crabbe*, which contains an interesting view of Harland and of his flat by the shabby, alienated 'Baron Corvo':

> Crabbe waited a couple of minutes in a large and very dainty drawing-room. There were a couch and a piano and lots of weird and comfy chairs, and a feminine atmosphere. Sidney Thorah [referred to in the novel as 'editor of *The Blue Volume*'] suddenly fell in, with a clatter and a rush; and began to talk-on-a-trot. He was a lank round-shouldered bony unhealthy personage, much given to crossing his legs when seated and to twisting nervously in his chair. He had insincere eyes, and long arms which dangled while he was silent and jerked and waved when he spoke. He spoke a great deal, in eager tones inlaid with a composite jargon which was basically Judisch but varied with gibberish of newly-arrived American students of the Latin Quarter. . . . His conversation was amazingly witty, pleasant, ephemeral, and insincere.[16]

Harland reportedly informed Rolfe that he would earn £700 on his second volume of *Stories Toto Told Me*, but Lane, on the following day, offered only £20 for the manuscript. This was not the first time that disagreements had arisen over money among publisher, editor, and author.[17] Despite misunderstandings, Harland and Rolfe became friends, and the 'Baron' was invited to Cromwell Road evenings, Ella D'Arcy recalling that he left 'singularly lively traces of his presence in Harland's armchairs.'[18] Rolfe, describing one such party, tells how Harland 'skipped and hovered and sat on his hind leg everywhere, like a cricket, a bluebottle, a toad clickety-clacking, buzzing, and rarely dumb.'[19] Rolfe, however, remaining silent, drank his tea and munched morosely on a bun. Producing a manuscript entitled 'About What is Due to Repentance,' included in the Toto stories, published in *The Butterfly* in August 1899, he handed it to Harland to read aloud. Present at this gathering was E. C. Stedman's son, Arthur, who, employed as a literary agent, wished to take a copy of the manuscript back with him to New York. Aline and Harland, when guests were leaving, offered Rolfe encouragement, but, according to Miriam Benkovitz, nothing came of the Harlands' gestures except 'poor advice and empty promises.'[20] However, when Rolfe's *In His Own Image* (1901) was in manuscript, it was dedicated, in part, to the Harlands 'in acknowledgment of hospitality.' When he read the manuscript for Lane, Harland urged Rolfe to remove a certain 'flavour' from it. As later depicted in *Nicholas Crabbe*, Rolfe insisted on clarification. Harland named it – pederasty :

> It came upon Crabbe like a clap of thunder, or the blast of some malignant star. His fierce claws quivered. He flamed in the face ; and went out, icily and indecisively.
> 'That's quite gratuitous. What a frightfully degenerate imagination you must have. Now mark me : I won't make, or permit to be made, a single alteration.'[21]

Harland responded that Rolfe was a 'fool,' and if he published the book as it stood, he would have to close his door to him. Convinced that the Harlands were determined to keep him in his 'mire of poverty,' Rolfe left in anger and later removed the Harlands' name from the dedication.

But this was not the end of their relationship, for at Christmas time in 1899 and 1900, Harland sent Rolfe a gift of £2.2.0.[22] Harland also welcomed him, in the morning, to his flat after Rolfe had walked from Hampstead through Hyde Park to South Kensington ; over breakfast, he would tell Harland of the Borgias, whose history he was writing. When *Chronicles of the House of Borgia* appeared in 1901, Harland wrote enthusiastically to 'Dear Corvo' : 'Your Borgia is GREAT. To say nothing of the labour and the learning of it – the historic imagination, the big vision, the humour, the irony, the wit, the perverseness, the daring, and the tremendously felicitous and effective *manner* of it ! ! It is like a magnifical series of tapestry pictures of the XV Century. Of course I think you are *advocatus Diaboli*, but *WHAT* an advocate. In any land save England, such a book would make its author at once FAMOUS and RICH. It is GREAT.'[23] Remarked Rolfe : 'This letter gains point from the fact that Mr Harland thus spontaneously exploded in a shriek of admiration after a personal and acerb disagreement of two years' duration.'[24] When he made application to the Royal Literary Fund early in 1902, Rolfe sent copies of his books and the letter of praise from Harland, which he characterised as a 'weird appreciation.'

After Harland read the manuscript of *Nicholas Crabbe*, Aline wrote to Lane on July 5, 1905, that in her husband's opinion Rolfe's novel was criminal libel, that its mailing to Lane constituted publication, and that Lane's solicitor must force Rolfe to admit his errors and promise never to repeat them. Lane immediately wrote to Rolfe, threatening him with a suit, but on July 7, Rolfe declared that his novel was a romance and that Lane and the Harlands had 'sniffed "lampoons & libels" where none are.'[25] This incident, we may assume, ended whatever remained of the friendship between Rolfe and the Harlands.

Through most of 1899, the Harlands were in France, where Harland worked on a new novel, to be entitled *A Precious*

Seeing (derived from Shakespeare's *Love's Labour's Lost*), but which was changed to *The Cardinal's Snuff-Box*. In a letter to Lane, he described the novel's setting as the 'Italian Lake Country' : 'It is all done in my best light conversational manner – like "Castles near Spain," "The Invisible Prince," &c.' In the same letter, he informs Lane that he has been 'seriously thinking of making a visit to America this autumn, as you have advised. Friends there tell me your advice is excellent – they promise that my old books *(Grey Roses* and *Comedies and Errors)* will take a new lease on life, and that the way will be prepared for my new one.' However, he needs money (£50 'on account') in order to pay 'certain pressing debts,' finish his novel, and make the trip to America in October : 'If not, I shall be interrupted and delayed in my work by financial worries – and I shall have to give up my trip to America, in order to save the tin for present emergencies.'[26]

While still in France, Harland followed the re-trial of Alfred Dreyfus at Rennes in September with particular interest. Dreyfus was again found guilty, this time under extenuating circumstances, and pardoned – a verdict that infuriated the Dreyfusards. Upon his return to Cromwell Road at the end of September, Harland wrote to Gosse : 'We were in France all through that dreadful trial, and read the *Figaro's* verbatim reports every day. We feel as if we should never wish to go to France again.'[27] Harland's reaction to the trial is important, in view of the anti-Semitic slurs in his later work. Such slurs were probably the result not of personal hatred but of widely held cultural attitudes towards Jews. That one who had had so many Jewish friends in New York and who welcomed to *The Yellow Book* and to his flat the writer Stanley V. Makower[28] should be so profoundly influenced by such attitudes is not especially enigmatic, for, as we have seen, his attitude towards Jews in the 1880s was quite ambivalent, and perhaps his progressive conservatism, in politics and religion, polarized his ambivalences more sharply. He regarded himself, he told an interviewer in 1903, as a 'bigoted Papist,' insisting that 'everybody else is, however, because we all are born so – only many of us don't know it'[29] – a characteristically shocking remark designed, perhaps, to startle readers.

That his outrage over the Dreyfus trial should involve the condemnation of his beloved France is an indication that his sense of justice had been deeply violated. Indeed, upon his return to London, he wrote a piece uncharacteristic of one who customarily avoided involvement in political and social issues. Appearing in *The Academy*, the article, entitled 'A Neighbourly Suggestion,' is an ironic proposal that France ought to be concerned with literature and art, where her genius lies, but allow the British to govern the country ('. . . we have never failed to do our work in masterly style. Look at India. Look at Egypt.') Harland's rhetorical strategy involves the creation of 'a friend' whose suggestion concerning Britain's management of French affairs, Harland believes, has merit. However, Harland concludes, the French are not likely to approve: 'What is the kink, the perversity, in their intelligence, which would prevent their seeing and accepting it?'[30]

In October, Harland responded to Lane's request to provide more information on his work in progress. On October 22, Harland provided more details on the characters, plot, and length; enthusiastically, he concludes his description of the novel: 'It ends HAPPILY. . . . It is full of colour, sparkle, atmosphere. . . . It's RIPPING.'[31] Lane, presumably without seeing the completed manuscript, sent him an 'acceptance' but without an advance. Wrote Harland: 'I have not the least idea what to do with this "acceptance." I have never had one before, and don't understand it. I think

I would rather have the cheque you spoke of. . . . Do send me a plain ordinary cheque then, and I will return this document.'³² But apparently Lane moved with caution and without any monetary commitment (despite Harland's protestations that he was 'stony-broke'). Meanwhile, Harland informed him that three other publishers were 'knocking at [his] door' : '. . . one of them has suggested a definite arrangement, which was rather dazzling.' However, Harland still preferred Lane as his publisher, expressing his preference in this same letter with deep-felt candour :

> . . . it would be a personal grief to me to leave the Bodley Head. You and I are, I hope, a good deal more to each other than mere publisher and author ; I hope we are very close and intimate old friends. It is a happiness to me to be one of the Bodleyans, and to be published by my friend – just as it would be a grief to me to go elsewhere. It would be the break off of an altogether charming tradition in my life, a beautiful continuous relation.

He concludes that therefore he cannot accept the proposals of other publishers. Still he 'must have money. And therefore I appeal to you to make a desperate effort to send me fifty pounds.'³³ Eventually, this crisis in their relationship was overcome, and Lane published the novel in May of 1900.

Before publication of *The Cardinal's Snuff-Box*, Gosse proposed in February that Harland do a critical introduction for a new translation of Octave Feuillet's novel, *The Romance of a Poor Young Man*, to appear in a series titled 'French Classical Romances,' that Gosse was editing. Writing to Gosse, Harland approved of the choice among Feuillet's works, for 'that is a book with which I have a hundred pleasant associations.'³⁴ He informs Gosse in the same letter that he will begin the introduction 'at once' (but which he would not be able to complete for some time) and tells him that he has just 'put the last touches' to the last page of proof of a novel he has been trying to write : 'I wonder whether you will think it a terrible example of what the novel should not be?'

When Harland saw the advance copies of the novel, he was deeply distressed by its appearance. To Chapman, he wrote :

> I cannot tell you how disgusted, how dismayed, I am at the appearance of *The Cardinal's Snuff-Box*. To say nothing of the very cheap and nasty effect of the binding, with its dull gilt lettering *un*incised, the machine-cutting of the pages simply gives the volume the effect of a thing written by Jerome K. Jerome. . . . The worst of it is that the better, the more cultivated English public will not buy a cut book.

He informed Chapman that the whole edition would have to be suppressed and a new one, uncut, in a decent binding, substituted for it (a naive request from an experienced, published author !). Harland was convinced that because of its appearance 'the failure of the book is assured beforehand.'[35]

Harland, however, had overestimated the effect of the appearance of his novel on the reading public and had underestimated the appeal to the general reader. On May 4, 1900, *The Cardinal's Snuff-Box* was published by Lane in both London and New York.[36] Calling it a prodigious success, Parry states that 100,000 copies were sold within two years, and *The Bookman* reported that Harland made $70,000 from royalties.[37] According to *The Critic*, the novel sold ten times more in America than it did in Britain ; thereby, Harland suffered a loss in royalties : 'He didn't bother about copyrighting it here, because to copyright a book in America it has to be put into type in America.'[38] Harland was so renowned that various publishers began re-issuing his early novels with his name preceding his pseudonym on the title page.

The phenomenal success of *The Cardinal's Snuff-Box* is

but another example of Harland's capacity to write a story calculated to please popular taste. In the novel, the romance between Peter Marchdale, a well-to-do Englishman living in Italy, whose novels are unread (again, Harland's obsession with the failed artist), and the Duchessa Beatrice, a beautiful Englishwoman, who is now a widow, is set in an idyllic, pastoral world where vulgarity and ugliness are excluded. Indeed, the only event in the novel is Beatrice's winning of Peter to the Roman Catholic Church with the help of her benevolent uncle, Cardinal Udeschini, whose snuff-box is a central device that brings about the conversion of the hero and his winning of the duchess, reminiscent of such devices in the nineteenth-century 'well-made play' by which conflicts were resolved. There is, however, little conflict in Harland's fantasy, and there is little wit ; coy dialogue abounds as well as predictable characterization and outcome. It is tempting to see Harland in Marchdale : both are writers and converts (and, indeed, Marchdale has used a pseudonym) ; the Cardinal refers to Marchdale's 'philosophic mind,' similar to a phrase used by Aline in accounting for her husband's conversion.[39]

The jarring note in the novel is the occasional anti-Semitic remark. In the context of Harland's romance, it strikes one as gratuitous but deeply felt, as though Harland could not contain it to preserve the essential nature of the world he has created. That world is succinctly described by Beatrice, who, sitting on a rustic bench at the riverside, says : 'What a sweetly pretty scene. Pastoral – idyllic – it reminds one of Theocritus – it reminds one of Watteau.' To give the following speech to Beatrice in her description of the history of the family castle is to introduce an element of ugliness into the romantic fantasy and into her character where none had existed before : 'The estate fell into the hands of the Jews, as everything more or less does sooner or later ; and they – if you can believe me – they were going to turn the castle into an hotel, into one of those monstrous modern hotels, for other Jews to come to, when I happened to hear of it, and bought it. Fancy turning that splendid old castle into a Jew-infested hotel!' (p. 311). Here Harland anticipates Wells in *Tono-Bungay* (1909), who describes the passing of the great country house, Bladesover, from the hands of English aristocracy to those of a German-Jew, with the resulting vulgarization of style and taste. For Wells, the opportunity for upward mobility is accompanied by the lamentable loss of an admirable way of life.

While correcting the final proofs of *The Cardinal's Snuff-Box*, Harland fell ill, and in the early summer, the Harlands left London for Italy and Switzerland, where they remained until the autumn. Writing to Gosse ('My dear Master') on July 5, from Lago Maggiore, Harland hoped that, by describing the countryside, Gosse would join them on his next holiday:

> I am looking at Mignon's island as I write – across half a mile of blue-green lake, it rises in a terraced garden, a formal Italian garden, filled with orange-trees and lemon-trees, with pomegranates and oleanders in flower, with thrushes and blackbirds and ring-doves. The ring-doves are wonderfully tame – they come up to within a yard of the British invader, and stare at him stupidly from their stupid little beady eyes. There are white peacocks in the garden too, though (alas!) there's no absinthe to feed 'em with.

The latter alludes to an anecdote told about Harland, who once taught a peacock at a café in the Bois de Boulogne to eat cake soaked in absinthe.[40] In his next novel, *The Lady Paramount*, Harland again alludes to the incident.

His letter continues with a vision of nature joined to the artifice of art, particularly that of the Pre-Raphaelites:

> And then our view – our view down and across the lake.

It's like the glorified drop-scene of a theatre in fairyland :
soft hills, backed by bolder mountains, covered by
forests and vineyards, dotted by toy-villages, and
bathed at all hours in the most beautiful, the most
improbable hazy lights – rose, mauve, violet, royal
blue, pearl-gray, gold, and silver.

Of his health, Harland writes at length, providing Gosse
with the essential reason why he has not completed the introduction to Feuillet :

I am getting better, I think, but, oh, so slowly. All night
long, night after night, it is cough, cough, cough, and
pain, pain, pain. But I am able to work a little every
morning now – so I suppose I am getting better. The
thing I'm working at is of course the Feuillet. I had just
begun it when the microbe struck me down, and it is
only now that he has allowed me to take it up again. I'm
afraid you'll think me a delinquent workman – but it's
really not my fault. Hang these microbes.[41]

By October, the Harlands had settled in Florence, having consulted doctors in Lucerne, who advised against returning to London. To Gosse, Harland wrote : 'Here I think we
shall stay until the weather or health or something makes a
further move imperative.'[42] Despite what Harland once
called the 'philistine' Cromwell Road, he lamented over his
isolation from London and the Gosses : 'But oh, and oh, and
oh, how we shall miss the smoke of the Cromwell Road and
our jaunts to Delamere Terrace and our heavenly evenings
there – with that most brilliant of talkers, and that most kind,
responsive, and witty of hostesses.'

Harland's health did not improve by December, for he
writes to Gosse that he has not been 'very well' but immediately adds that he has been 'overwhelmingly busy.' Again,
he urges Gosse to join them : 'And whatever Florence has in
the way of English-speaking society would of course be at
your feet – though I'm afraid you'd find it a sufficiently

uninteresting foot-stool, the people here are so heroically dull.' Sympathizing with him on the recent loss of his step-mother, Harland refers to Gosses's devotion to her and the fortune that he has justly inherited, adding : 'It is a disgrace to England (and America – to Anglo-Saxon-dom, in fact) that the higher and more scholarly branches of the literary craft should be so ill-remunerated as to give a man no ghost of a chance to *save*. I wonder, though ,whether they manage these things much better in France?'[43]

The Harlands returned to London probably early in 1901, when Harland was at work on his next novel. They apparently spent part of that year in France, for Aline writes that 'a good portion of *The Lady Paramount* was written at beautiful, suggestive Versailles, and in Paris.'[44] The title of the novel was derived from *The Cardinal's Snuff-Box*, where Peter Marchdale speculates that the beautiful Italian villa and estate belong to 'the lady paramount of this demesne.' Harland used the title to suggest to his readers a continuation of the sort of fantasy he had offered before. Aline, whose judgments of her husband's work reveal steadfast devotion rather than critical acumen, later wrote of this novel : 'The style of *The Lady Paramount* is, it has often been declared, simple inimitable. The grace, buoyancy, mirth, irresponsi-bility, with which its pages teem, – and they do lightly play upon eternal verities, – make it distinctly Henry Harland's *chef d'oeuvre* . . . the book is quite unique, unparalleled in English prose.'[45] But, of course, *The Lady Paramount* does have its parallel in *The Cardinal's Snuff-Box*, since both depict similar worlds and similar romances that make little pretence to psychological realism.

Published in April, 1902, *The Lady Paramount* con-tains familiar plot situations and the guaranteed happy ending that had made *The Cardinal's Snuff-Box* such an extraordin-ary success. The 'Lady Paramount' is Susanna, Countess of

Sampaolo, a small island off the Italian coast. Believing that her English cousin, Anthony Craford, whom she has never seen, is the true heir to her estates, she goes to England to meet him – of course, in true Harland style, concealing her identity. The inevitable occurs : he falls in love with her, and he promises that he will visit Sampaolo. Eventually, he discovers what the reader has known all along – that Susanna and the Countess of Sampaolo are the same person. There is little left for Anthony to do but assume the title and marry the Countess.

The novel contains many allusions and motifs that reveal Harland's obsessions and sensibility. The central theme of the novel – the restoration of a title to the rightful heir – recalls Harland's search for a titled ancestor in his own family. Interestingly, Aline later referred to her husband as 'Sir Henry Anthony Harland,' apparently borrowing the middle name after the hero of *The Lady Paramount*. In the novel, Anthony says to Susanna: 'I am glad to note that in politics you are a true-blue reactionary.' Harland depicts Anthony and Adrian Willes as dandies, whose conversational exchanges are presumably designed to recall Restoration drama or Wilde's *The Importance of Being Earnest*. Unfortunately, the wit is tepid, and Adrian, the more flamboyant and debonair of the two, uses lines from Shakespeare and other writers to enhance his sophistication. The occasional anti-Semitic remark seems remarkably consistent in this world, when Adrian, a composer of songs, says: 'I make [music] as the bee makes honey, as the Jew makes money, spontaneously, inevitably.' In addition, there are references to the beauty of Catholic ritual, and even a reference to Harland himself, when one of the characters, a Miss Sandus, tells Susanna of a literary man who had once taught a peacock to eat sponge-cake soaked in absinthe. When Susanna asks what happened to the 'poor peacock,' Miss Sandus replies :

'When you're married and come to stay with me in Kensington, I'll ask the literary man to dinner.'

The critical reception of the novel was generally quite favourable, especially in America, but *The Academy* was quite adversely critical: 'The book discloses quite plainly the boundary of Mr Harland's range. . . . He never relies successfully on the fundamental unassisted force of imagination. And further, his inventive power resembles his heroine in waywardness. When it fails him, he is a ruined author.'[46] In the *Catholic World*, however, a study of Harland's work by the Rev. John J. Burke reports that 'some who are now Catholics were first led to think well of the church by the reading of Mr Henry Harland's *The Cardinal's Snuff-Box*.' In *The Lady Paramount*, Rev. Burke points to the continuing interest in Catholicism and concludes: 'His work above all else is throughout clean, wholesome, and elevating.'[47]

In the same year, Feuillet's *The Romance of a Poor Young Man* appeared with Harland's critical introduction. In asking Harland to write it, Gosse evidently believed that Feuillet would be of particular interest to him, for *The Romance of a Poor Young Man* resembles Harland's Anglo-Italian romances. In Feuillet, there are figures who are of noble blood, and there is the wooing and winning by the hero of an aristocratic lady of great beauty. Harland's introduction provides insight into his own literary practices, when, for example, he writes: 'To be serious seriously is the way of mediocrity. To be serious gaily is not such an easy matter. . . . Olympus laughs because it perceives so many capital reasons for pulling a long face; and half the time pulls a long face simply to keep from laughing. I imagine it is in some measure the olympian mannner of seeing which explains the gay seriousness of the work of Octave Feuillet.'[48] And Harland praises Feuillet's heroines, who are 'always womanly' and 'almost always religious.'

In December, 1902, Harland, after more than thirteen years abroad, returned to America, according to one interviewer, 'after a very stormy passage on *La Champagne*.'[49] For most of 1903, Harland spent his time between New York and Norwich, where, at Sentry Hill, he stayed with his mother and his uncle, General Harland. Regarded widely as an eminently successful novelist now returned in triumph, he was interviewed for newspapers and magazines. Maintaining his poise and pose, he provided, as we have seen, many details about his life that became standardized errors for years to come. To one interviewer, he said : 'I write novels because it's more sport than fox-hunting.' Asked what impressed him about New York since his departure, he replied with characteristic levity that it was the squirrels : 'There is nothing like them in London or in any foreign city I know of. . . . I shall miss the pretty things when I go away.' He insisted that he had returned to America 'just to see Norwich again.' Asked whether it was his birthplace, Harland replied : 'By the merest accident, not. But I won't tell you where I was born, because I've made up my mind that I was born in Norwich. At all events I wanted to be born there and it's an aggravation to me to think that I wasn't. So I don't think it. . . . Any biographer of mine who says that I was born elsewhere than in Norwich, Conn., makes a mistake – though technically he may be correct. Norwich is the Rose of New England. In fact it is the Rose of the World. Of course there are London and Paris and Vienna and Rome and other large cities, but they are merely satellites of Norwich.'[50]

During his stay in America, Harland serialized his next novel, *My Friend Prospero*, in *McClure's Magazine*.[51] In addition to completing it at Sentry Hill, Harland also supervised the rebuilding of the estate ; indeed, the Harlands 'took a very great delight' in improving 'the picturesque old place,' as Aline later wrote. 'The ancient stone terraces were reset ;

the lawns rolled and trimmed, the grounds extended, the gardens enlarged.'[52] Writing to Witter Bynner, Harland asked him whether he was coming to Norwich during the summer: 'Come and help me "farm." All the afternoon you will find me in the fields, followed by twelve assistants, trying to improve the face of this old estate.'[53] According to Louise Howe, it was an estate of 'magnificent elms; its terraced gardens were full of flowers from the time the first snowdrops and daffodils bloomed until the frost blighted the last asters and chrysanthemums. Behind the gardens on the hill, where Harland Place now stands, were orchards and pastures where cows grazed, and from the summer house on the hill-top there was a wide view of river and hills.'[54]

The young Miss Howe spent much time at Sentry Hill in 1903, and her memories of her friendship with the Harlands provide an interesting view of that year in America. Curiously, Harland, who reportedly was once disturbed when it was mentioned that he spoke English with an American accent, seems to have rediscovered his American heritage at Sentry Hill:

> There we often walked, Harry and Aline and I, and he would go into rhapsodies over the view, the trees, everything connected with his ancestral home, which he loved so dearly. But once I remember in the early spring he found a little hawthorn tree struggling to live in a sheltered corner of that bleak hill-top and his joy was boundless. It was to him the choicest thing on the place, a reminder of his beloved England, for which he was beginning to grow homesick.

Miss Howe refers to his poor health but also to his personal vitality:

> Henry Harland had the most vivid personality of anyone I ever knew. He was brilliant, witty, whimsical and sarcastic, sometimes quite maddening, but always unique and interesting. I can see him now striding up

and down the drawing room on winter afternoons when we were having tea, pouring out a perfect stream of brilliant conversation. No one else dared break into that monologue, but we sat about and listened in delight. Sometimes he would try out on us bits of what he was writing. Afterwards we would recognize whole pages in *My Friend Prospero*. . . .

Because of his health, Harland's doctors urged him to go to Colorado, or, if he must go abroad, to Switzerland. Bynner recalls meeting Harland in New York after the consultation with the doctors, whose advice had saddened him, for he was reluctant to go to the West, where life would be 'intolerably bleak' among people so different from his customary circle of friends. 'His final retort I shall always remember,' writes Bynner, 'as a flash of genuine bravado. . . .': 'Give me death with dutchesses [*sic*].'[55]

But it was more than just the city of London that he yearned for. When interviewed in December, 1903, in New York, he stated that the chief advantage of a residence in England for a writer is that 'he there hears the language which he writes spoken by living people all about him. In other words, he is writing a living language, as it is spoken by the people best fitted to know how to speak it, and therefore as it should be written. You in America, for instance, have only a transplanted English, a sort of foreign importation, as it were, of the mother tongue.' Clearly facetious in his remarks about language, Harland delighted in asserting the presumed superiority of British English:

> Any language which is not spoken, but is studied at the schools and universities, is a dead language and therefore the Americans who write good English – and I suppose there must be some Americans who do write good English – are writing in a language as dead to them as Latin and Greek. Now, how could I, therefore, as a student, a writer of English, live in America? I wish to

write in a living language and I must live where that language lives. I fancy a year on end in New York might remove one's ability to write English at all.[56]

In January, 1904, while the Harlands were still in America, *My Friend Prospero* was published in book form. Designed to please his readers, the ingredients are similar to his previous Anglo-Italian stories (as though predicting its oblivion, one periodical reported that the novel was without a single 'unpleasant' incident and that it ended happily).[57] The setting is familiar : an estate in Lombardy with a castle, formal garden, terraced lawns, cypresses, fountains, statues, balustrades (one wonders whether Harland wished to remodel Sentry Hill after the settings of his novels). The hero, presumably a cobbler's son, is in reality the heir to an English peerage ; and a miller's daughter is, in fact, of Austrian nobility. The outcome of this fairy tale is highly predictable, as is the preoccupation with Catholicism and with Jews. When, for example, Lady Blanchemain, a sort of fairy godmother who attempts to unite the two branches of a family long divided by a feud, persuades the hero, who has lived in Italy, to accompany her to London for the 'season,' he asks : '. . . there's a liberal scattering, I've heard, of Jews ?' To which she replies : 'Oh, Jews are all right – when they aren't Jewy.' The little girl with a symbolic name, Annunziata, embodies Harland's mystical faith, but he fails to develop her sufficientlyfor her to emerge as a really striking creation or a convincing symbolic presence. Interestingly, Harland introduces an American character named Winthrop, descended from a colonial family ; he is, moreover, a baronet and a Catholic convert (Harland cannot, it appears, resist his own fantasies).

My Friend Prospero had a phenomenally good sale. *The Bookman* (New York) reported, in its survey of best-selling books in 1904, that Harland's novel was in eighth place for the year ; in May of that year, it had risen to fourth place. The article is illustrated with the pictures of eight best-selling authors, including Ellen Glasgow and Winston Churchill. Though John Lane not unkindly wrote that Harland's 'charming love romances' are now 'the delight of millions,'[58] some reviewers were growing tired of Harland's formula for fiction. Wrote one : '. . . *My Friend Prospero* would be bettered by more vertebrae.'[59] Soon after the novel appeared, Reggie Turner wrote to Max Beerbohm : 'Have you read the Harland book yet? Even the reviewers seem to recognise the story. He will have to invent another plot.'[60] But though such criticism was growing, Harland was nevertheless regarded as an important novelist. Archibald Henderson, a distinguished academic critic who was later Shaw's biographer, regarded *My Friend Prospero* as one of the three most significant American books of the past six months despite the fact, as he wrote, that *The Cardinal's Snuff-Box, The Lady Paramount,* and *My Friend Prospero* 'have the same plot, the same situations, and almost the same characters.'[61]

In February, 1904, the Harlands left New York on board the R.M.S. *Ivernia* for England. Aline's letter, written en route, reveals to Stedman ('Dear Godfather of Harry')[62] the uncertainties that faced them in the future. The sun she writes, is 'flooding the row of deck-chairs and their occupiers and tries to persuade us the Riviera could not be better. But *I* know better, and I am not inspired, and am very low in my mind at parting from all the darling people that America holds.' Stedman had written to her, apparently, about their plans, for Aline responds to his query : 'We never make plans but plans have made us, for owing to the necessary break with Lane's publishing firm in America which took place before we left, Harry has got to rush on with his novel to appear serially in *McClure's,* and he finds he works best in his own habitat in London.' The difficulty may have been with the firm's failure to give Harland an accounting of royalties, a problem which Aline discusses later in her letter in connection with her husband's other publishers. The allusion to the current novel in progress for *McClure's Magazine* is, of course, *The Royal End*, which Harland never lived to complete.

In the same letter, Aline reveals their plan to return to Connecticut : '... [Harry] has promised that in July we shall come again and spend the summer in Norwich ... and I can have my father near me there. ....' Indeed, their plans were to spend part of their time every year in 'God's Country' : 'Nothing would make me happier. And some day I should not be surprised if, when the present novel is finished, the greatest American novelist should try his pen at the greatest American novel. New England has seized upon him. It became very nearly a possession while he was in Norwich.' As for Stedman's advice that Harland ask for an accounting of royalties from various publishers that had handled his books in America, Aline reports : 'The sum they said they owed him, 160 dollars or thereabouts, was for a year. But Harry had had no account rendered him for those books for the past 10 years. He wrote requesting they would send their account for that time, and having no reply he has put the matter in his lawyer's hands with the papers relating to it.' Aline concludes her letter with a comic flourish by saluting Stedman : 'Oh Grand Romantique, Premier Gentilhomme d'Amérique' : 'The spring tulips and hyacinths were only symbols of your eternal sympathy. ....'[63]

Once back in London, Harland found that he would need a milder climate. The Harlands consequently spent part of 1904 in San Remo, where, in October, Howells visited them with his wife. Howells wrote to his sister on October 16 that he was pleased with the climate, 'so much more tropical than Venice that it seems as if I had never been in Italy before.'[64] On January 9, 1905, Howells wrote from San Remo to a friend : 'A light of a certain sort of romance, but a very good, sick fellow, Henry Harland, is here, trying to heal his poor lungs, and really helping them.'[65] Howells returned to America in the spring of 1905, never to see Harland again. During this time, McClure also visited Harland, but not having seen his old friend for several years, he was shocked when he saw Harland without moustache and beard. When he asked why the moustache had been shaved off, Harland replied: 'Sam, the darned thing was getting white!'[66]

The salubrious air of San Remo gave Harland strength enough to return to England in the spring of 1905, when C. Lewis Hind saw the Harlands at the Mitre Hotel, Hampton Court, sitting in the sun by the river. Harland, though so thin that it was painful for Hind to look at him, was, in his talk, as 'fierce and volatile as ever.'[67] Early in the summer, however, Harland suffered a series of haemorrhages and was taken by his mother (who arrived in June), Aline, and a nurse back to San Remo in October. In late November, they took a villa, where he regained sufficient strength to rise early, stroll in the garden, where he would pick 'one lovely rose to lay on Aline's piano,'[68] and then spend the morning writing, pausing only to drink the milk outside his door. In the afternoon, he would spend time with friends and visitors.

On November 20, his mother wrote to Louise Howe: 'You can understand that I have been greatly preoccupied and absorbed in my poor boy's condition. Alas I still am, for he is no better – but I cannot speak of it. God alone knows the end. Life here at San Remo goes on much as life goes on everywhere. Harry & Aline having been here a good deal, have many friends among the English people here, and so there are a good many calls to be made & cups of tea to be disposed of.' After chatting about mutual friends in Norwich, Mrs Harland concludes her letter with a disturbing postscript: 'Pray for me & mine & love me all you can, for my heart is full of trouble.'[69]

The end came rapidly. Harland's health worsened by mid-December; on December 20, he died at the age of forty-four, with his mother and Aline at his side. On December 30, Aline wrote to tell Gosse of her husband's last days in a letter filled with grief but with a striking dignity and eloquence of expression:

Villa Solaro
San Remo, Dec. 30, 1905

My dear Mr Gosse:

I thank you for your most beautiful and kind letter. My love, my darling died, having received the Blessed Sacrament from the hands of his friend, Father von Egloffstein, with a radiant face.

A week before, his nerves gave way under the intolerable suffering caused by the fever and which had been his portion for months. After that, his strength ebbed and ebbed, though the doctors hoped almost to the last his wonderful vitality would prevail and that the crisis would pass, but he never rallied, his strength was sapped by the too long strain of suffering borne heroically since the seventh of June last.

Yet *I could not believe* he would die – when they told me that last morning he could not pass the day, the shock was as terrible as though they had brought him in stricken to death from a state of health. *He longed so to live!* To do yet more beautiful work. And though we sometimes wept upon each other's hearts in moments of discouragement, yet when the morning began, with sunshine here, and colour and the glow of Southern warmth and,[70] as it did often, with a fairly moderate degree of fever, we would both again be filled with hope and joy. He would often have me place his manuscripts and pen and ink where he could see them, and would say: 'Tomorrow, I will begin to work. I have been lazy too long. Oh, shall I ever know the joy again of sitting down to my work, of writing, of chiselling beautiful sentences?' And he would make a motion of his hand, lovingly, like that of the sculptor tenderly modeling the curve of flesh in the clay.[71]

That last week, he was delirious at times but so *sweetly*, so beautifully. And then he would revive, and sit up, and talk so enchantingly that we were astonished, and the doctors would sometimes stay an hour, unable to go away. He had his full consciousness all of the last day, but he was so weak he could scarcely speak. He laid his head upon my head with love, such love, and pity.....

He was spared at least this. He did not have to live through what I lived through and which has *turned me into a stone*. He did not have to see *me* pass through the awful gate of Death. He did not have to live on with this desolation, with this loathing and disgust of everything.

I was not alone. My father was here, before we reached San Remo, and Mrs Harland had come, in response to a telegramme, the first haemorrhage, on the seventh of June. Every English speaking soul in San Remo loved Harry. The very servants came to beg permission to watch or pray by his bed. We took this villa with its big garden for him, exactly one month before the day he died. He lived in it exactly one month to a day. Yet it is full of him. I cannot leave it yet.

Goodbye. God bless you all. The wreath, the most lovely wreath, is there, where he is resting. He was buried on Saturday morning, December 23rd, from the little Mortuary Chapel of the Cemetery, which to its very portals overflowed with friends. The Mass for the dead was celebrated by his friend Father v. Egloffstein, whose tears fell upon the Altar.

He loved you all, and you will never know a soul more tender and loyal in friendship.

Always your
Aline Harland[72]

Epilogue

T HE REACTION TO Harland's death was, for the most part, respectful and appropriate. *The Athenaeum*, for example, wrote that he would be 'remembered by his exquisite accomplishment in a small compass' and that 'he had known his limitations better than his critics.'[1] Stedman, upon reading the news, pasted an obituary notice in his diary and wrote next to it: 'Too bad! too bad! My brilliant, beloved godson & pupil.'[2] Informed of Harland's passing, Henry James wrote to Aline on December 21, 'Don't think of him too wretchedly, for the *bitterness* of woe should be only for those who have missed life. He didn't do that – he had it, truly, almost all, and he knew, gallantly. . . .'[3]

On March 1, 1906, on what would have been Harland's forty-fifth birthday, his body was reinterred in consecrated ground at Yantic Cemetery in Norwich Town (Aline accompanied the coffin on the long journey fron San Remo). On March 3, Aline, in a letter to Stedman, recalled her 'little one, so glorious and so great, the martyr of pain during one whole terrible year': 'The very flesh of my heart, spiritual and physical, was torn out of it the day I left my love's room. The torture of the fourteen days at sea, God and he only know. But now, I think he is glad. The Mystery, the strange, dear, heavenly Mystery of it all. . . .' She urges Stedman to visit her at Sentry Hill: 'Together we will walk over these dear hills and through those woods which he carried in his heart, always. Oh, if we had never left them . . . this might not have happened. I cannot feel otherwise though when we went away, he wanted and needed to go, it was always with the idea that we were coming back, probably in a year to live here, more and more. You know he lived by love. And his heart was here . . . in this holy home.' Ending her letter, she quotes from Stedman's letter to her : 'You said so wonderfully, he was [one] of those "who should have died hereafter," yet thank God, not. For he *lives* more greatly, more gloriously, and eternally.'[4]

At the time of his death, Harland was completing a novel, *The Royal End*, a title he had already selected. In 1907, Stedman informed Gilder, of the *Century Magazine*, 'confidentially,' of the uncompleted manuscript. The editor, in turn, wrote to Aline enquiring about it, which he characterized, in its unfinished state, as 'a great handicap editorially and commercially,' adding : 'I can not say how great a loss it is that the exquisite art of the author did not have its full accomplishment in this work.'[5] Aline, however, had already decided to complete the manuscript with the advice of Gosse ; she wrote to Gilder that she was 'hard at work' on it : 'I feel with [Gosse] that the four parts make such a complete tale in Harry's most beautiful and lofty mood. The subtitle, An Italian Episode, can be added to explain and justify its publication as it stands.'[6] By December, Aline was still convinced that she wished to publish only the Italian episode of *The Royal End*. She had her husband's notes with which to complete the novel, but apparently she believed that it ought to end with his prose, not hers. She wrote to Gilder :

> Even now – although I don't quite agree with you and think the American episode [which Aline completed] *supremely* true – (it is necessarily in marked contrast to the Italian, is not the return to America

133

always the return to prose, for us all – after Italy ?). Yet – I still should very much prefer to publish the Italian episode serially and leave all the rest to the imagination of the reader.[7]

The Royal End, even with Aline's hand, is perhaps Harland's most interesting novel, certainly his most Jamesian effort, for it contains the story of a displaced American young woman who has lived in Europe since childhood and who discovers, eventually, her own displacement. Her return to New England to claim her heritage is symbolically the story of Harland himself, whose return to Norwich in 1903 resulted in a psychological transformation that he had not anticipated. The usual Harland elements are here : characters move with 'languid grace' and aphorisms abound (better, for the most part, than in previous novels) ; there are also the Catholic allusions and the occasional anti-Semitic slur. The heroine, Ruth Adgate even talks like Harland : 'I'm always sincere – but seldom serious. What's the good of being serious ? Isn't levity the soul of wit ? Come, come ! Life's grim enough, in all conscience, without making it worse by being serious.' When she returns to New England, the name of her ancestral home, Barracks Hill, recalls Sentry Hill, and the description of the estate reinforces the parallel ; indeed, Ruth improves the surrounding acres by cutting paths through the woods and enlarging the flower gardens, much as Harland had relandscaped Sentry Hill.

The opening of the novel in Venice is particularly impressive in its structural complexity. A principal character, Prince Bertram, the exiled ruler of a small Italian state, eventually becomes associated with Ruth and her friends, Lucilla and Harry Pontycraft, brother and sister, both English, who accompany her on an unending leisurely tour of Europe. They are all exiles, both forced and voluntary, in the shadowy world of Venice, described impressionistically — taking its inspiration from Arthur Symons and looking forward to T. S. Eliot in *The Wasteland*: '. . . before them rose the domes and palaces of Venice, pale and luminous, with purple blacknesses of shadow, unreal, mysterious, dream-compelling, as a city built of cloud.' The novel, however, falls into two distinct parts and styles, and the American episode, if, indeed, Aline followed her husband's notes, is distinctly a lessening of tension and interest.

The Royal End appeared in February, 1909, while Aline was travelling abroad (indeed, she wandered restlessly for years after her husband's death). On March 6, she wrote to Louise Howe from on board the *Cedric* in Naples : 'The town spreading out below . . . and the blue Mediterranean and all the blue bay of Naples flashing in the sunlight, and my heart faints with joy. For I look on the things which Harry and I have seen together ; I live the life which Harry and I lived together. I love the God which Harry and I loved together, and Harry and I seem at last very near to the portals of Heaven.'[8] On April 23, she writes from Fiesole that she is worried 'about the two at Sentry Hill,' an allusion to Harland's mother and General Harland. She suddenly interrupts her letter with 'Dear Harry !. . . . Where are you ?'[9]

Two months later, she writes to 'Our dear Mother and Uncle Ned' from England of a visit to Salisbury to see the Maurice Hewletts, who showed her their splendid home and gardens, an experience that profoundly depressed her :

> We had tea under a splendid cedar – and cigarettes of course. Lots of talk – and then I was dragged off to see the Rock Garden and the bridge and the brook through their grounds and all the wonderful things which they have done in five years. Ah me ! Then I began to feel that life wasn't worth living and all I wanted was to turn my face to the wall and weep myself to death.

Aline's preoccupation with death and loss, observable here, is echoed further in her letter when she states that, after returning to London, she went to dinner 'among my Gallery of Dead Ladies. . . . I knew very well that I was, also, a "dead lady" and that this indeed was just the place for me.' Curiously, she suddenly writes about herself and Harland as though he were still alive : 'And when Harry and I went in, to the Chapel after dinner, and felt that sweet flowing love of the Blessed Sacrament, once more, after three days, — I realized that it is better to be a Dead Lady with God and Harry, than a living one without either.'[10]

In June, 1910, she writes to Miss Howe from the Hotel Buckingham in New York about the splendid weather : 'It's like walking in Heaven with my boy today.' And during the winter of 1910-11, she wrote several more letters from the same hotel in which her obsession with the memory of her husband and her comfort in knowing that he dwells in Heaven are central. In one letter, she remarks : 'No one has ever been so amusing as Harry. No one ever will be so amusing as Harry unless he comes again to Earth. I expect the Saints chuckle the whole day long, in whatever part of Heaven he finds himself.[11]

Her instability worsened about the time of the First World War, for she began signing her letters 'Aline, Lady Harland' and she referred to her husband as 'Sir Henry Harland' in letters to publishers and literary agents. Her calling cards announced her as 'Lady Henry Harland,'[12] and Louise Howe, who 'kept in touch with Aline until she got completely unlike her old self,' writes that Aline once registered in a Norwich hotel as 'Lady Harland,' to the 'astonishment of the proprietor.'[13] Harland's fantasies in his Anglo-Italian novels had indeed become a reality to Aline, and his interest in the possibility of a lost title in the Harland family now became fully realized in his wife's dream world.

In 1917, Aline published privately a play written by her husband and Hubert Crackanthorpe, titled *The Light Sovereign*, a work obviously written for their own amusement. Time should have mercifully obliterated it, for it contains slender wit and witless plot. In a letter to Louise Howe in 1911, Aline apparently alludes to it: 'I am re-reading the most amusing play of Harry's, which keeps me in a state of mirth and joy – and when it's finished I begin it over again.'[14] What amused her so much is difficult to see, except for one or two lines. The play combined Harland's interest in royalty and revolutionaries, with Latin Quarter Bohemians, such as 'Bodley Head, an English poet, slightly decadent' and 'Popoff,' a revolutionary. At one point, one character says of French novels: 'I'd rather die than read one. Their horrid yellow covers are enough. Yellow is such an unblushing colour. A yellow book is sure to be immoral.'

'Always more or less a creature of moods,'[15] Aline suffered from further mental deterioration in the 1920s.[16] By the 1930s, she required hospitalization in Pilgrim State Hospital (now known as Pilgrim Psychiatric Center) in Brentwood, Long Island, in the State of New York, where she died on August 27, 1939. Hospital records list her as an 'authoress' and the widow of 'Sir Henry Harland.'[17] On August 31, she was interred beside her husband at Yantic Cemetery. None of the Norwich newspapers carried an obituary or notice of her burial.

Aline's death ended her extraordinary devotion to her husband's memory and to his artistry that lived, as she said, 'more greatly, more gloriously and eternally' in death.

Stedman's words of consolation to Aline in 1906 that Harland's name and work 'will not die' were, however, a limited prophecy. Some of his works have indeed been reprinted since his death, but only one, *The Cardinal's Snuff-Box*, his best-known novel, has been issued in ten different editions (the last, in paperback, in 1946). In America, six Harland titles were in print in 1977, provided by commercial reprint houses primarily for libraries; in Britain, however, there were none. Harland's name, unknown to the general reading public, is known only to scholars specializing in late nineteenth-century literature.

What was the extraordinary appeal that once attracted such great numbers of readers to Harland's later novels and stories? Essentially, it was the creation of an imaginative world that appealed to those who sought a refuge from political and social crises, from increasing materialism and secularism, for Harland created an idyllic landscape of unerring romance in which aristocrats, committed to the old religious faith, find happiness in a world free of unseemly passion and ugliness. Often involving a farcical drama of wit and masks, such a mythical earthly paradise of privilege and benevolence inevitably inspired admiration and longing.

Harland's mythologized world – in which he himself appears in suitably artistic disguise – seems to have developed from his fear of failure (an obsessive theme in his work). Henry James, we recall, sensed that in 1893 Harland was deeply disturbed because of his 'literary longings unaccompanied by the *faculty*.' Possibly, Harland also felt that the failure of *The Yellow Book* was, in part, his responsibility. His romantic sentimentality, as evidenced in stories during *The Yellow Book* period and later in his novels, reveals a pressing need for an imaginative world capable of transcending the existing world of fact, with its danger of failure. However, his obsessions with artistocracy (his figures are invariably benevolent, witty, and mysterious) and a pastoral, innocent view of their world imposed severe restrictions upon his artistic resourcefulness (only in his final novel, *The Royal End*, did he seem to strike a new, interesting chord).

138

Yet Harland, in his earlier work, revealed a potential that seemed to be halted mid-way in his career. His technique of recovering lost experience through the device of involuntary memory, which Proust was later to exploit, might have led to important work. 'Incurably romantic,' Harland chose to write sensational novels, and later he adopted his sterile mode of pastoral sentimentality. Because popularity was essential to him as a measure of artistic success (despite his admiration of James), he consequently developed singularly identifiable plots and characters that attracted a wide audience.

Harland may still be read with pleasure, especially in such stories as 'Tirala-tirala' and 'When I Am King,' and such earlier sensational novels as *As It Was Written* and *Two Women Or One?*. An intense, devoted writer, Harland attempted, perhaps too self-consciously, to create significant literary works, convinced that 'perfection' of style was of central importance. But as an artist, he lacked the mysterious alchemy that enduring art requires. His fame ultimately rests upon his editorship of *The Yellow Book*, which, with its broad spectrum of artistic endeavour, remains the quintessence of the 1890s.

His friendships with most of the leading artists of his time reveal an extraordinarily engaging personality, whose wit and vitality impressed all who knew him. Though Harland's life was not one of disorder or aberration, he nevertheless deserves mention among those whom Yeats designated as 'The Tragic Generation.' Like Yeats's tragic figures, who walked 'upon a rope, tightly stretched through serene air,'[18] Harland strove in his brief, intense life for personal and artistic transcendence in a world of fragmentation and incoherence.

Source Notes

Abbreviations and Names Cited

Glastonbury	G. Glastonbury, 'The Life and Writings of Henry Harland,' *Irish Monthly*, April, 1911, pp. 210-19.
JM	*Jewish Messenger* (New York)
Mix	Katherine L. Mix, *A Study in Yellow: The Yellow Book and Its Contributors* (Lawrence, Kansas & London, 1960).
NB	*Norwich Bulletin*
NYPL	New York Public Library
SR	*Saturday Review*
Stedman and Gould	Laura Stedman and George M. Gould, *Life and Letters of Edmund Clarence Stedman*, 2 vols. (New York, 1910).
YB	*Yellow Book*

[Transcripts of autograph letters are designated as 'TS.' Consult section III of the Bibliography for a full listing of locations of Henry and Aline Harland's correspondence. All titles of books and periodicals referred to in correspondence have been shown in italics.]

ONE

1. Stedman to Aline Harland, March 1, 1906, TS., Columbia.
2. Le Gallienne, *The Romantic '90s* (London, 1951), p. 136.
3. Symons, 'The History of the *Yellow Book*,' unpub. TS., Univ. of Texas.
4. Bynner to Roberts, October 10, 1927, Harvard. Bynner met Harland in 1903 through their family connections in Norwich. Curiously, Aline Harland, in her article on her husband, gives his date of birth but not his birthplace *(See* Glastonbury, p. 211). Harland's obituary in the New York *World*, December 22, 1905, p. 9, gives his birthplace as Brooklyn, and *The Reader* (Indianapolis), Sept., 1906, p. 442, also gives the same birthplace.
5. Donald A. Roberts cites the U.S. Census for 1870, Schedule I, listing inhabitants in the 11th District, 20th Ward in the County of New York, as evidence that Harland was born at 178 Fourth Street. *See* 'Henry Harland: The Luska Phase,' unpub. M.A. thesis, Columbia University, 1928, p. 9. However, there is no record of Harland's birth in the Municipal Archives for Manhattan, which does contain ledgers listing births in 1861.
6. Stedman and Gould, I, p. 156.
7. Ibid., p. 177.

8. *See* obituary of Irene Harland, *NB*, January 21, 1925, p. 5; George E. MacDonald, *Fifty Years of Free-Thought* (New York, 1929), I, pp. 260-62.

9. Inscriptions on the gravestones of the children in Yantic Cemetery, Norwich Town, are as follows: Thomas Harland (December 23, 1863 – February 18, 1871); Caroline Ruth Harland (October 1865-May 5, 1866).

10. *See* obituary, *NB*, March 10, 1915, p. 5.

11. Margaret Fuller, *A New England Childhood* (Boston, 1916), p. 87. The 2,000 volumes were donated to Connecticut College, New London, by Henry's mother in 1915-16.

12. Albert Parry, 'Henry Harland: Expatriate,' *The Bookman* (New York), Jan., 1933, p. 2.

13. 'Our Own Times,' *The Reader*, Sept., 1906, p. 442.

14. Glastonbury, p. 211.

15. Ibid., p. 211.

16. *See* Donald A. Roberts, 'Henry Harland, '82 – College Years,' *City College Alumnus* (New York), Feb.-March, 1930, pp. 23-4.

17. Beekman Place, between East 49th and 51st Streets, was named after a prominent Dutch family that had settled in colonial New Amsterdam (later New York). Mount Pleasant, a mansion built by James Beekman in 1763 at 51st Street and the East River, was used by Lord Howe as head-quarters during the American Revolution when the British occupied Manhattan in 1776. It was demolished in 1874. In his early novels, Harland always gave fictitious numbers in Beekman Place, whose highest number, at least today, is 39.

18. Roberts, 'Henry Harland, '82 – College Years,' p. 23.

19. Stedman and Gould, v. II, p. 382.

20. Harland's registration card, in the Alumni Record Office, Harvard. What he studied as a student is unknown.

21. Letter from her daughter to Donald A. Roberts, cited in 'Henry Harland: The Luska Phase,' p. 16.

22. Information from 'a lady who desires to remain anonymous,' cited by Roberts, p. 17.

23. Letter from the daughter of the pastor, Rev. James Eddy, November 8, 1927, cited by Roberts, p. 34.

24. 'Mr Henry Harland,' *New York Herald*, December 13, 1903, Third Section, pp. 4-5.

25. Gustave Kobbé, 'Timely Interviews,' *The Lamp* (New York), New Series, April, 1903, p. 225. Harland's trip abroad after leaving Harvard is confirmed by Aline Harland. *See* Glastonbury, p. 211.

26. Wilde, 'The Critic as Artist,' *Complete Works of Oscar Wilde*, ed. J. .B. Foreman (London, 1970), p. 389.

27. Letter from Zinnser to Donald A. Roberts, November 16, 1927, cited in 'Henry Harland: The Luska Phase,' p. 18.

28. Parry, 'Henry Harland: Expatriate,' p. 3.

29. Arthur Stedman, 'An American Author Abroad,' *Philadelphia Press*, August 5, 1894, p. 28.

30. Glastonbury, p. 211.
31. When he resigned a year later, Harland was earning $150 a month. *See* 'Record of Vouchers for Salaries, City and County of New York,' Finance Department, New York City, 1883-86.
32. *See* Glastonbury, p. 211. The time of Harland's rising differs in some accounts.
33. *Grandison Mather* (New York, 1889), p. 272.
34. See *Merriam Genealogy in England and America*, comp. Charles Henry Pope (Boston, 1906), p. 323.

TWO

1. Harland to Stedman, April 17, 1885, TS., Columbia.
2. Stedman Diaries, Columbia.
3. Harland to Stedman, April 17, 1885, TS., Columbia.
4. Harland to Stedman, April 18, 1885, Columbia.
5. TS., Stedman Papers, Columbia. The Stedman papers contain only a transcription of the inscription, not the book itself.
6. Notes written by Louise Howe, TS., Stanford.
7. Notes written by Laura Stedman, Stedman Papers, Columbia.
8. *Grandison Mather*, p. 288.
9. Stedman and Gould, II, p. 358. On June 4, Harland informed Stedman that Dunham had offered a royalty on all copies sold after the first 500 (in the late nineteenth century, royalties, instead of outright payment for a manuscript, were a relatively new procedure), but Harland complained of the appearance of a novel published by Cassell: 'It was forbidding. I think to put a book in such a binding is, so far as readers of good taste are concerned, equivalent to putting it into its tomb.' Harland to Stedman, June 4, 1885, Loyola.
10. An allusion to Lady Augusta Noel's *From Generation to Generation* (London, 1879).
11. Quoted in Roberts, 'Henry Harland: The Luska Phase,' p. 28.
12. Justin O'Brien, 'Henry Harland, an American Forerunner of Proust,' *Modern Language Notes* (Baltimore), June, 1939, pp. 420-28.
13. *As It Was Written* (New York, 1885), p. 26.
14. Roberts, 'Henry Harland, '82 — College Years,' p. 23.
15. John J. Clarke, 'Henry Harland: A Critical Biography,' unpub. doctoral dissertation, Brown University, 1957, pp. 18-19.
16. *JM*, September 25, 1885, p. 5.
17. *As It Was Written*, pp. 105-06.
18. 'A Purim Episode,' *JM*, December 11, 1885, p. 9.
19. *See* E. K. Brown, *Willa Cather: A Critical Biography*, completed by Leon Edel (New York, 1953), p. 182.
20. S. S. McClure, *My Autobiography* (London, 1914), p. 177.
21. Harland to McClure, November 25, 1885, Columbia.
22. Harland to Stedman, November 26 [1885], Columbia.
23. Harland to Stedman, December 5 [1885], Columbia. McClure discusses his long friendship with Harland in his autobiography but makes no mention of their early conflict.

24. 'A Half-Score New Novelists,' *Atlantic Monthly* (Boston), Feb., 1886, p. 261.
25. Harland to Wendell, September 17, 1885, Harvard.
26. Ibid. Harland wrote: 'I am hard at work now, trying to finish up novel number two. I have already "contracted" for it with the publishers.'
27. 'The Lounger,' *The Critic* (New York), March 27, 1886, pp. 156-57. *See* 'Notes About Authors,' *The Book-Buyer* (New York), New Series, Jan., 1886, p. 395.
28. *Mrs Peixada* (New York, 1886), pp. 100-01.
29. Ibid., p. 102.
30. 'New Books,' *New York Times*, April 5, 1886, p. 3.
31. Arthur Bartlett Maurice, *New York in Fiction* (New York, 1901), pp. 69-70. This volume contains interesting photographs of some of the buildings in the Beekman Place neighbourhood where Harland set his early novels.
32. *The Critic*, April 10, 1886, p. 180.
33. 'Editor's Study,' *Harper's New Monthly Magazine* (New York), July, 1886, p. 314.
34. Stedman recorded the Harlands' expected departure in his diary on May 7, 1886. Stedman Diaries, Columbia.
35. Harland to Stedman, July 1, 1886, Boston Public Library. Stedman had reservations about the novel when he read it in manuscript: 'It is stronger, better, but unfortunately more sensational than "As It Was Written." ' Diary, November 12, 1885, Columbia.
36. The Torah, referring to the first five books of the Old Testament (also called the 'Pentateuch') is not today spelled with the additional 'h.'
37. Harland to Stedman, June 4, 1886, Boston Public Library.
38. Harland to Stedman, September 7, 1886, Columbia.
39. Harland to Steadman, July 28, 1886, California.
40. Harland to Stedman, June 20 [1886], Boston Public Library.
41. Ibid.
42. *The Yoke of the Thorah* (New York, 1887), p. 171.
43. Ibid., p. 177.
44. *JM*, July 8, 1887, p. 4.
45. 'Open Letter,' *JM*, July 22, 1887, p. 1.
46. *JM*, November 4, 1887, p. 4. The story that Harland defended himself by appearing at one of the city's synagogues to deliver a talk is told by William H. Carpenter, 'The Editor of "The Yellow Book," ' *The Bookman* (New York), March, 1895, p. 88. However, I have seen no evidence to support it.
47. Harland's *My Uncle Florimond* was serialized in *Wide Awake* (Boston) from December, 1887 to May, 1887.
48. Harland to Howells, September 3, 1887, Harvard.
49. Harland to Howells, August 3, 1887, Harvard.
50. David Cheshire and Malcolm Bradbury, 'American Realism and the Romance of Europe: Fuller, Frederic, Harland,' *Perspectives in American History* (Cambridge, Mass., 1970), v. IV, pp. 285-310.
51. Harland to Webb, March 30 [1888], Library of Congress. Aline's uncle, Augustus C. Merriam (d. 1895), was a professor of Greek at Columbia University.

52. For Moore's slighting remarks about Howells, see his *Confessions of a Young Man*, ed. Susan Dick (Montreal & London, 1972), pp. 152-53.
53. Harland to Mrs Howells, November 27 [1888], Harvard.
54. Harland to Daly, January 7, 1889, Folger.
55. Parry, *Garrets and Pretenders: A History of Bohemianism in America* (New York, 1933), p. 76.
56. Harland to Stedman, April 20 [1889], Boston Public Library.
57. 'Recent Fiction,' *The Critic*, May 11, 1889, p. 233.
58. 'Editor's Study,' *Harper's New Monthly Magazine*, May, 1889, p. 987.
59. Stedman and Gould, II, pp. 358-59.
60. Sharp, 'New Novels,' *The Academy*, Nov. 30, 1889, p. 352.
61. Harland to Stoddart, June 7, 1889, Free Library of Philadelphia.
62. Harland to Stedman, July 13, 1889, Boston Public Library.
63. Harland to Howells, July 13, 1889, Harvard.
64. Stedman Diaries, July 17, 1889, Columbia.

THREE

1. Harland to Stedman, August 16, 1889, TS., Columbia.
2. Aline Harland to the Stedmans, November 12, 1889, Columbia.
3. Harland to Howells, December 30, 1889, Harvard.
4. McClure, *My Autobiography*, pp. 178-79.
5. Waugh, *One Man's Road* (London, 1931), p. 214.
6. Glastonbury, p. 212.
7. Harland to Unwin, October 18, 1901, Berg Collection, NYPL.
8. In his introduction to the translation, Gosse calls Matilde Serao (1856-1927) 'the most imaginative novelist of the latest generation in Italy.' In 1894, Aline published a translation of Serao's novel *Farewell, Love* for the same series.
9. Waugh, *One Man's Road*, pp. 213-14.
10. Ibid., p. 295.
11. Richard Watson Gilder (1844-1909), a poet, was the editor of the *Century Magazine* (New York).
12. Harland to Stedman, December 24, 1900, Columbia.
13. 'Novels of the Week' *The Athenaeum*, May 16, 1891, p. 632.
14. Paul F. Mattheisen and Michael Millgate, eds., *Transatlantic Dialogue: Selected American Correspondence of Edmund Gosse* (Austin, Texas & London, 1965), pp. 200-01. The autograph letter, with the added date of July 2, 1891 written by another hand in pencil, is in the Rutgers University Library.
15. Aline Harland to Mrs Stedman, September 4, 1892, Columbia.
16. Ibid.
17. Harland to Stedman, November 18 [1892], Columbia.
18. Harland published three stories in *Black and White*: 'A Light Sovereign,' September 10, 1892, pp. 304-08, rpt. in *Mademoiselle Miss* (1893); 'A Re-incarnation,' June 10, 1893, pp. 706-08, rpt. in *Grey Roses* (1895); and 'The Prodigal Father,' Dec. 30, 1893, pp. 838-42, rpt. in *Mademoiselle Miss* (1893).
19. Gosse, 'A First Sight of Verlaine,' *The Savoy*, April, 1896, pp. 113-16;

rpt. in Gosse's *French Profiles* (London, 1905), pp. 182-88.

20. Harland to Gosse, [April, 1893], Rutgers.
21. James to Gosse, *Letters of Henry James*, ed. Percy Lubbock (New York, 1920), v. I, p. 203.
22. Harland to Gosse, May 11, 1893, Rutgers.
23. Harland to Stedman, May 22 [1893], TS., Columbia.
24. Ibid.
25. *See* D. S. MacColl, 'Memories of the Nineties,' *London Mercury*, Jan., 1939, pp. 287-96; Alfred Thornton, 'Diary of an Art Student of the Nineties,' *The Artist*, April. 1935, pp. 53-54.
26. MacColl, p. 289.
27. Ibid., p. 290.
28. Aline Harland to Stedman, August 31 [1893], Columbia.
29. Quoted in Mix, p. 65.
30. Aline Harland to Stedman, August 31 [1893], Columbia.
31. *The Century Guild Hobby Horse* (later *The Hobby Horse*) had, of course, first appeared in 1886, but it was limited in its appeal. MacColl had apparently suggested a periodical for a much wider audience.
32. Mabel Beardsley and her mother visited the GROB, and with the Harlands and others sent a comic summons to Beardsley to join them. *See* Margery Ross, ed., *Robert Ross: Friend of Friends* (London, 1952), p. 34. (The date of the summons as given in the text is erroneous: it should be 1893, not 1894.)
33. *See* Beardsley's letter to Robert Ross, dated late November, 1893, in *The Letters of Aubrey Beardsley*, ed. Henry Maas, J. L. Duncan, and W. G. Good (London, 1970), p. 58.
34. 'Mr Henry Harland,' *New York Herald*, December 13, 1903. Third Section, p. 4.
35. Beerbohm, *Letters to Reggie*, ed. Rupert Hart-Davis (London, 1964), p. 88.
36. *See* Waugh, *One Man's Road*, p. 250.
37. Waugh, 'London Letter,' *The Critic*, Jan. 20, 1894, pp. 42-43.
38. Waugh, *One Man's Road*, pp. 250-51.
39. *Letters of Aubrey Bearsley*, ed. Maas, *et al.*, p. 61.
40. A persistently erroneous view may be seen, for example, in William York Tindall's statement that *The Yellow Book* 'was intended to organize the decadence.' *See* Tindall, *Forces in Modern British Literature, 1885-1956* (New York, 1956), p. 24.

FOUR

1. According to Aline Harland, Beardsley proposed the title. *See* Glastonbury p. 214.
2. Waugh, *One Man's Road*, p. 252.
3. James, 'Preface' to Vol. 15, *The Novels and Tales of Henry James* (New York, 1909,) p. vi.
4. Quoted from a conversation between Ella D'Arcy and Katherine L. Mix cited in Mix, p. 190.
5. Harland to Garnett, June 2, 1896, Univ. of Texas.

6. Harland to Lane, June 15 [1894], Westfield.
7. Harland to Lane, undated, Westfield.
8. Harland to Le Gallienne, undated, Yale.
9. D'Arcy to Katherine L. Mix, November 11, 1935, Penn. State.
10. *See* Harland to Lane, June 15 [1894], Westfield.
11. For Vol. II, Harland did not pay Beerbohm for his 'Letter to the Editor.' *See* Harland to Lane, June 12, 1894, Westfield.
12. Nelson, *The Early Nineties: A View from the Bodley Head* (Cambridge, Mass., 1971), p. 300.
13. Ibid., p. 300.
14. Harland to Waugh, February 1, 1894, Boston Univ.
15. Le Gallienne, *The Romantic '90s*, p. 59.
16. Ibid., pp. 136-37. A similar picture of Harland's work habits is given by Laura Stedman in unpublished notes prepared in 1928 (Stedman Papers, Columbia): 'Telling me how he caught the first morning impressions, when all was fresh, simply had his coffee, *read nothing* until after his stint of creative writing. Then his papers and letters, etc. But the morning hours were devoted to his work, would not even dress, so as not to waste an atom of that fresh vigour & strength. He felt that most important fact as to the quality of the *Cardinal's Snuff-Box*, etc.'
17. Aline Harland to Stedman, undated, Columbia.
18. Margaret Fuller to Katherine L. Mix, Feb. 5, 1947, Stanford; quoted in Mix, p. 61.
19. *The Yoke of the Thorah*, pp. 260-61. Ethel Colburn Mayne, writing of evenings spent in Cromwell Road, recalls Harland's enthusiasm in 'reading, declaiming, quoting, almost breathing Browning! It was from Henry Harland that this reader learnt to read *The Ring and the Book.*' *Browning's Heroines* (London, 1913), p. viii.
20. The volume, including (in addition to Harland) such figures as Mark Twain, Theodore Roosevelt, Frank R. Stockton, Stedman, and Howells, was designed to raise funds for a library and furnishings in its new quarters.
21. Harland to Le Gallienne, February 2 [1895?], Univ. of Texas.
22. Harland to Lane, [late 1894], Westfield.
23. Harland to Lane, postmarked March 19, 1885, Westfield.
24. Harland to Lane, undated, Westfield.
25. Lane, *Aubrey Beardsley and The Yellow Book* (London & New York, 1903), pp. 5-6.
26. Waugh, 'London Letter,' *The Critic*, April 28, 1894, p. 290.
27. May, *John Lane and the Nineties* (London, 1936), p. 74.
28. Aline Harland to Stedman, May 21, 1894, TS., Columbia.
29. Waugh, 'London Letter,' *The Critic*, May 5, 1894, p. 312.
30. A day before publication of *The Yellow Book*, James wrote to Gosse: '. . . on the launch of the Yellow Book – its apparent prospects or possibilities. Does Harland droop? – or swoop?' James to Gosse, April 15, 1894, Duke Univ.
31. Waugh, *One Man's Road*, p. 255.
32. Pennell, *The Life and Letters of Joseph Pennell* (Boston, 1929), vol. I, p. 273.

33. Mathews to Brushfield, February 7, 1895, Univ. of Reading; partly quoted in Nelson, *The Early Nineties*, p. 271.
34. 'A Yellow Melancholy,' *The Speaker*, April 28, 1894, pp. 468-69.
35. Harland to Lane, undated, Westfield. In the same letter, Harland adds: 'I'll bet you a shilling George Moore wrote the *Speaker* notice.' However, Edwin Gilcher's *Bibliography of George Moore* (DeKalb, Ill., 1970) does not list it.
36. *Letters of Aubrey Beardsley*, ed. Maas *et al.*, p. 68.
37. *Letters of Henry James*, ed. Lubbock, v. I, pp. 216-17.
38. John M. Richards, *The Life of John Oliver Hobbes* (London, 1911), p. 86.
39. Michael Field, 'Days and Years,' diary entry dated April 17, 1894, partly unpublished manuscript in the British Library. John Singer Sargent wrote to Gosse: 'From an aesthetic point of view I dislike that book too much to be willing to seem an habitual contributor.' *See* Evan Charteris, *John Sargent* (London, 1927), p. 142.
40. Harland to Lane, undated, Westfield.
41. Aline Harland to Stedman, May 21, 1894, TS., Columbia.
42. Harland to Lane, June 12, 1894, Westfield.
43. Lane's notes, Princeton Univ. For the published version, *see* his *Aubrey Beardsley and The Yellow Book*, pp. 4-5.
44. Hamerton, 'The Yellow Book: A Criticism of Volume I,' *YB*, July, 1894, p. 181.
45. Harland to Le Gallienne, [October, 1894], Univ. of Texas; printed, with several errors in transcription in Le Gallienne's *The Romantic '90s*, pp. 138-39.
46. Le Gallienne, 'Paris Day by Day: A Familiar Epistle,' *Robert Louis Stevenson: An Elegy and Other Poems* (London, 1895), p. 29.
47. Harland to Le Gallienne, Feb. 2 [1894?], Univ. of Texas.
48. 'A Yellow Bore,' *The Critic*, Nov. 10, 1894, p. 316.
49. Harland, 'When I Am King,' *YB*, Oct., 1894, p. 72.
50. Evelyn Sharp, *Unfinished Adventure* (London, 1933), pp. 57-60.
51. Hind, *Naphtali*, (London, 1926), p. 90.
52. Beerbohm to Ross in *Robert Ross*, p. 44.
53. Quoted in Patrick Chalmers, *Kenneth Grahame* (London, 1933), p. 66.
54. Syrett, *The Sheltering Tree* (London, 1939), p. 77.
55. Derek Patmore, *Portrait of My Family* (London, 1935), p. 225.
56. Viola Meynell, *Alice Meynell* (London, 1929), pp. 72-73.
57. Mix, p. 136. Harland asked Arthur Symons to request a contribution from Walter Pater, who replied that he was too busy at the moment. In the same year, he died. See *The Letters of Walter Pater*, ed. Lawrence Evans (Oxford, 1970), pp. 147-48.
58. Harland to Lane, Oct. 22 [1895], Westfield.
59. Ibid. The writer was H. D. Lowry.
60. Stanley Weintraub, *Aubrey Beardsley: Imp of the Perverse* (University Park, Pa. & London, 1976), pp. 126-29.
61. *A Leaf from the Yellow Book: The Correspondence of George Egerton*, ed. Terence de Vere White (London, 1958), p. 38.
62. Mattheisen and Millgate, eds., *Transatlantic Dialogue*, p. 231. For

Harland's view of Wilde and 'the story of his ruin,' see the same letter. In April, 1898, a year after Wilde's release from prison, the Harlands dined with him in Paris, and when *The Ballad of Reading Gaol* appeared, Wilde instructed his publisher to send a copy to Harland. See *Letters of Oscar Wilde*, ed. Rupert Hart-Davis (London, 1962), pp. 700, 731.

63. Quoted from a conversation between Ella D'Arcy and Katherine L. Mix, cited in Mix, p. 145.
64. Harland to Chapman, undated, Westfield.
65. Mabel Kitcat, 'Henry Harland in London,' *The Bookman*, August, 1909, p. 610.
66. 'A Bookman's Table,' *The Bookman*, July, 1895, p. 423.
67. Harland to Le Gallienne, Feb. 2 [1895], Univ. of Texas.
68. Le Gallienne, *Retrospective Reviews* (London: John Lane, and New York: Dodd, Mead, 1896), v. II, p. 259.
69. Harris, 'Three Yellow Book Story-Tellers,' *SR*, June 1, 1895, pp. 730-31. The review is unsigned.
70. Malcolm Elwin, *Old Gods Falling* (London, 1939), p. 341.
71. Harland to Lane, July 11 [1895], Westfield.
72. Ibid.
73. Harland to Lane, [probably July 14, 1895], Westfield.
74. Weeks, *Corvo* (London, 1971), p. 117.
75. *See* Weeks, p. 188.
76. 'A Letter . . . from the Yellow Dwarf,' *YB*, Oct., 1895, p. 131.
77. Harris, 'Chronicle,' *SR*, Nov. 2, 1895, p. 567.
78. *SR*, Nov. 9, 1895, p. 603.
79. Waugh, 'London Letter,' *The Critic*, Nov. 30, 1895, p. 374.
80. There is no evidence that Harland's family was related to Admiral Robert Harland (1715-84), created 1st Baronet in 1771 for his service to the Crown. Sir Robert had one son(1765-1848), who became 2nd Baronet, but since he was childless, the title became extinct upon his death. *See* G. E. C[okayne], *Complete Baronetage* (Exeter, 1906), v. V, p. 155.
81. Waugh, 'London Letter,' *The Critic*, Nov. 30, 1895, p. 374.
82. *The Memoirs of Arthur Symons*, ed. Karl Beckson (University Park, Pa. & London, 1977), p. 170.
83. Custance, Diaries, 1894-99, Berg Collection, NYPL.
84. The eight letters, all undated, are in the Berg Collection, NYPL.
85. Quoted in Mix, p. 63.
86. 'Lounger,' *The Critic*, Jan. 9, 1897, p. 27.
87. Symons, 'Literary Causerie: By Way of Epilogue,' *The Savoy*, Dec., 1896, p. 92.
88. *The Times*, January 29, 1897, p. 14.
89. 'Chronicle and Comment,' *The Bookman*, July, 1896, p. 391.
90. Glastonbury, p. 215.
91. Quoted from conversation between Ella D'Arcy and Katherine L. Mix, cited in Mix, p. 274.
92. Ibid.
93. In addition to his stories and 'Yellow Dwarf' letters, Harland, according to Ella D'Arcy, published a story in *The Yellow Book* under a pseudonym,

'Robert Shews': 'The Elsingfords,' Oct., 1896. *See* Mix, p. 230. D'Arcy also informed Mix that Aline Harland had contributed two stories under a pseudonym, 'Renée de Coutans': 'A Lady Loved a Rose,' July, 1896, and 'Natalie,' Jan. 1897. Mix to Karl Beckson, Sept. 22, 1977.

94. Beerbohm to Katherine L. Mix, cited in Mix, p. 62; Beerbohm, *Seven Men* (London, 1919), p. 19.

95. Kitcat, 'Henry Harland in London,' p. 60.

FIVE

1. Harland to Lane, undated, Westfield.
2. Harland, 'O.S.,' *The Academy*, April 24, 1897, pp. 453-54.
3. Harland, 'Concerning the Short Story,' *The Academy*, June 5, 1897, pp. 6-7.
4. 'Mr Henry Harland,' *New York Herald*, December 13, 1903, p. 4.
5. Stedman and Gould, v. II, pp. 251-52. A previously planned trip to America in September, 1895, referred to in a letter from Harland to Lane, dated August 20 [1895], Westfield, did not materialize.
6. Harland to Gosse, [early Jan., 1898], Cambridge.
7. Harland to Lane, undated, Westfield.
8. Parry, 'Henry Harland: Expatriate,' p. 8.
9. James, 'The Story-Teller at Large: Mr Henry Harland,' *Fortnightly Review*, 1898, pp. 650-54. Leon Edel has written that James considered Harland the 'supreme case not of the expatriate – that was himself – but of the dispatriate,' for Harland had cut himself off from America. *See* Edel, *Henry James: The Master, 1901-1916* (London, 1972), p. 388.
10. Obituary of Henry Harland, *The Times*, Dec. 22, 1905, p. 10.
11. Harland to Gosse, undated, Rutgers.
12. Harland, 'Mr Henry James,' *The Academy*, Nov. 26, 1898, pp. 339-40.
13. Edel, *Henry James: The Master*, p. 388.
14. Glastonbury, p. 216.
15. Harland, 'Aubrey Beardsley,' *The Academy*, Dec. 10, 1898, pp. 437-38.
16. Rolfe, *Nicholas Crabbe* (London, 1958), p. 27.
17. In late 1895, Rolfe had written to Harland enquiring about payment for Toto stories published in the October volume of *The Yellow Book*. Harland, in turn, wrote to Lane: 'I have just had a very funny and rather pathetic letter from Baron Corvo, saying that he is abominably hard up, and asking whether he mayn't have a cheque for his tales in the last *Y.B.* without waiting months, and whether you cannot be persuaded to make it for £10:10:0. We had marked him for £7 I think.' Harland to Lane, undated, Westfield. Rolfe, impatient, then wrote directly to Lane claiming that Harland had not paid him. See *Without Prejudice: One Hundred Letters to John Lane*, ed. Cecil Woolf (London, 1963), p. 14.
18. Quoted in Miriam Benkovitz, *Frederick Rolfe, Baron Corvo: A Biography* (London, 1977), pp. 113-14.
19. *Nicholas Crabbe*, p. 42. Aline (called 'Eileen') is described as 'a dark pale tired timid little thing, with a secret and the voice of a nightingale.'
20. Benkovitz, p. 114.
21. *Nicholas Crabbe*, p. 119.

22. Benkovitz, p. 137.
23. Rolfe, *Letters to Grant Richards* (St. Ives, 1952), pp. 43-44.
24. Weeks, *Corvo*, p. 195.
25. Benkovitz, p. 171.
26. Harland to Lane, Aug. 12 [1899], Westfield.
27. Harland to Gosse, Sept. 30 [1899], Rutgers.
28. For an account of Stanley V. Makower (1871-1911), see Frederick Whyte, *A Bachelor's London* (London, 1931), pp. 227-31.
29. Kobbé, 'Timely Interviews,' *The Lamp*, April, 1903, p. 226.
30. Harland, 'A Neighbourly Suggestion,' *The Academy*, Oct. 22, 1898, p. 124.
31. Harland to Lane, Oct. 22 [1899], Westfield.
32. Harland to Lane, undated, Westfield.
33. Harland to Lane, undated, Westfield.
34. Mattheisen and Millgate, eds., *Transatlantic Dialogue*, pp. 243-44.
35. Harland to Chapman, undated, Westfield.
36. On April 25, 1900, shortly before the publication of *The Cardinal's Snuff-Box*, Harland's father, Tom, died of pneumonia in a hospital on Staten Island, New York. Associated with the law firm of Rollins & Rollins at the time of his death, Tom Harland, wrote the *New York Daily Tribune* on April 26, 1900, was 'a man of great learning and intellectual power and active in their exercise to the very end of his life.'
37. Parry, 'Henry Harland: Expatriate,' p. 10; 'Chronicle and Comment,' *The Bookman*, Feb., 1906, p. 552.
38. 'The Lounger,' *The Critic*, April, 1902, p. 306. According to *The Critic*, Harland, because he did not like the American way of spelling, did not permit the novel to be copyrighted in America, since that would have required it to be put into type there.
39. Aline Harland used the phrase 'metaphysical mind.' Glastonbury, p, 216.
40. Elizabeth Robins Pennell, *Nights* (Philadelphia & London, 1916), p. 265.
41. Harland to Gosse, July 5 [1900], Rutgers.
42. Harland to Gosse, Oct. 19 [1900], Rutgers.
43. Harland to Gosse, Dec. 9 [1900], Rutgers.
44. Glastonbury, p. 216.
45. Ibid.
46. 'Popularity,' *The Academy and Literature*, May 3, 1902, pp. 459-60.
47. Rev. John J. Burke, 'Mr Henry Harland's Novels,' *Catholic World* (New York), June, 1902, pp. 398-403.
48. Harland, 'Introduction' to Octave Feuillet, *The Romance of a Poor Young Man*, trans. C. G. Compton (London, 1902), p. v.
49. E. F. Harkins, *Little Pilgrimages*, Second Series (Boston, 1903), p. 201.
50. Kobbé, 'Timely Interviews,' *The Lamp*, April, 1903, p. 225. In a letter to Lane, Harland wrote of New York: 'We are almost dead of the NOISE and confusion of this noisy, confused, but most hospitable town.' Harland to Lane, Dec. 19, 1902, Westfield.
51. In a letter (no addressee is given), Harland revealed that McClure was paying him $10,000 for American serial rights and an advance of $10,000

on a royalty of 20% for American book rights. For British serial rights, he was receiving £800, and for British book rights (advance on a royalty of 25%), Lane was paying him £1,000. Letter dated Aug. 1, 1903, Loyola.

52. Glastonbury, p. 216.
53. Harland to Bynner, undated, Harvard.
54. Notes written by Louise Howe, TS., Stanford.
55. Bynner to Donald A. Roberts, Oct. 10, 1927, Harvard.
56. 'Mr Henry Harland,' *New York Herald*, Dec. 13, 1903, p. 5.
57. 'The Church in Fiction,' *Catholic Book Notes*, June 10, 1904, p. 163.
58. Lane, *Aubrey Beardsley and The Yellow Book*, p. 7.
59. Eleanor Hoyt, 'Current Fiction,' *The Lamp*, March, 1904, pp. 154-55.
60. Turner to Beerbohm, [March, 1904], Harvard.
61. Henderson, 'Recent Novels of Note,' *Sewanee Review* (Sewanee, Tenn.), Oct., 1904, pp. 456-58.
62. In September, 1903, Stedman had lunch with the Harlands, General Harland presiding, in Norwich. Recording the 'pleasant reunion' in his diary on September 10, Stedman wrote:'Talked with H.H. of his literary plans. He now can make at least $20,000 a year, & has brilliantly fulfilled my beliefs of 20 years ago.' Stedman Diaries, Columbia.
63. Aline Harland to Stedman, Feb. 19, 1904, Columbia. In dating her letter, Aline inadvertently wrote '1903' instead of '1904.'
64. Howells, *Life in Letters of William Dean Howells*, ed. Mildred Howells (New York, 1928), v. II, p. 202.
65. Ibid., p. 205.
66. McClure, *My Autobiography*, p. 179.
67. Hind, *Naphtali*, p. 90.
68. Notes written by Louise Howe, TS., Stanford.
69. Mrs Thomas Harland to Louise Howe, Nov. 20, 1905, TS., Stanford.
70. At the foot of the page, Aline wrote:'The first page was blotted with tears. I have had to rewrite it—'
71. For Aline's later version of this scene, *See* Glastonbury, p. 219.
72. Aline Harland to Gosse, Dec. 30, 1905, Leeds.

EPILOGUE

1. Obituary of Henry Harland, *The Athenaeum*, Dec. 30, 1905, p. 898.
2. Stedman Diary, Dec. 21, 1905, Columbia. On December 22, Lane wrote to Stedman that he was 'terribly shocked' at the news of Harland's death: 'I knew he had been seriously ill, yet I cannot realise the truth of it. I knew him so intimately; during the days of the *Yellow Book* I saw him daily and grew to love him very much.' Lane to Stedman, Dec. 22, 1905, Columbia.
3. James to Aline Harland, Dec. 21, 1905, Harvard.
4. Aline Harland to Stedman, March 3, 1906, Columbia.
5. Gilder to Aline Harland, July 10, 1907, MS. Div., NYPL.
6. Aline Harland to Gilder, July 31 [1907], MS. Div., NYPL.
7. Aline Harland to Gilder, Dec. 10, 1907, MS. Div., NYPL.
8. Aline Harland to Louise Howe, March 9, 1909, TS., Stanford.
9. Aline Harland to Howe, April 23, 1909, TS., Stanford.

10. Aline Harland to Mrs Thomas Harland and Edward Harland, June 26, 1909, TS., Stanford.
11. Letters to Louise Howe, TSS., Stanford.
12. Printed calling card, Aline Harland Papers, Connecticut College, New London.
13. Louise Howe to Katherine L. Mix, undated, Stanford.
14. Aline Harland to Howe, Jan, 2, 1911, TS., Stanford.
15. Louise Howe to Katherine L. Mix, undated, Stanford.
16. Much correspondence to Margaret Fuller has survived. It deals principally with Aline's instructions to her concerning the sale of stocks and bonds located in a safety deposit box in a Norwich bank of which General Harland had been president. Fuller had, for years, tried to follow Aline's detailed and complicated directions. Finally, in a letter to Aline, Fuller wrote on April 26, 1923: 'Now, my dear Lady Harland, I must ask to be excused from further correspondence. I have gone as far as I can, and farther than I would have gone for almost anyone else.' At the foot of this typewritten letter, she added in her own hand: 'Lady Harland enclosed no postage whatever for her letters which I was to forward & have forwarded to Norwich, France, Eng., and Italy. I have paid long distance telephone charges, and other charges, & registered letters galore, also insurance & bank charges.' Aline Harland Papers, Connecticut College.
17. Clarke, 'Henry Harland: A Critical Biography,' p. 364. The hospital has declined to give any information about Aline Harland, but apparently gave John J. Clarke these few facts in 1957.
18. Yeats, *Autobiographies*, London, 1926, p. 373.

Bibliography

The following numbers are used with titles to identify Harland's pseudonym and his own name (sometimes appearing in parentheses beneath the pseudonym, sometimes vice versa) as they appear on the title page of each work:

  1 — Sidney Luska
  2 — Sidney Luska (Henry Harland)
  3 — Henry Harland (Sidney Luska)

* — An asterisk indicates that the volume has not been personally examined. No identification number is given to titles published under his real name.

I The Works of Henry Harland

1 *As It Was Written: A Jewish Musician's Story.*¹ New York, Cassell, [1885].

1a — London, Cassell, [1885].

1b — ¹ New York, Cassell, [1887]. *Cassell's Rainbow* series, Vol. 1, No. 3.*

1c — ² New York, Street & Smith, (1900), *Romance* series No. 4.*

2 *Mrs Peixada*¹ New York, Cassell, (1886).

2a — ¹ New York, Cassell, (1888). *Rainbow* series, Vol. 1, No. 22.*

2b — ¹ New York, Street & Smith, (1901).*

3 *The Yoke of the Thorah.*¹ London, Cassell, [1887].

3a — ¹ New York, Cassell, (1887).*

3b — ² New York, Street & Smith (1900). *Romance* series, No. 2.*

4 *My Uncle Florimond.*² Boston, Lothrop, (1888). (Serialized in *Wide Awake* (Boston), December, 1887-May, 1888).*

5 *A Latin-Quarter Courtship and Other Stories.*² New York, Cassell [1889]. (Contains 'A Latin-Quarter Courtship,' 'Mr Sonnenschein's Inheritance,' 'Lilith,' and 'Mr Ormizon's Dinner Party.')

5a — New York, Street & Smith, [1901].*

6 *Grandison Mather; or an Account of the Fortunes of Mr and Mrs Thomas Gardiner.*² New York, Cassell, [1889].

6a — ² New York, Street & Smith (1900). *Romance* series, No. 7.*

6b — ² London, Cassell [1890].

7 *Two Women or One? From the Mss. of Dr. Leonard Benary.*³ New York, Cassell, [1890].

7a — London, Cassell, 1890.

8 *Two Voices.*³ New York, Cassell [1890]. (Contains 'Dies Irae' and 'De Profundis').

9 *Fantasy*, London, Heinemann, 1890. *Heinemann's International Library* Series. (Matilde Serao's novel translated by Henry Harland and Paul Sylvester from the Italian original).

9a — ³ New York, United States Book Co., [1890]. (The American edition does not give the name of Paul Sylvester as co-translator and spells the first name of Harland's pseudonym, appearing in parenthesis beneath his own name, as 'Sydney').

9b — [3] New York, J. W. Lovell, 1890.

10 *Mea Culpa: A Woman's Last Word.* London, Heinemann, 1891. 3 vols.

10a — [3] New York, J. W. Lovell, (1891).

10b — [3] New York, Street & Smith, (1901).

11 *Mademoiselle Miss and Other Stories.* London, Heinemann, 1893. (Contains 'Mademoiselle Miss,' 'The Funeral March of a Marionette,' 'The Prodigal Father,' 'A Sleeveless Errand' and 'A Light Sovereign').

11a — New York, Lovell, Coryell & Co., (1893).*

11b — London, John Lane, 1903. New edition with a brief introduction by the author.

12 *Grey Roses.* London, John Lane; Boston, Roberts Bros., 1895. Vol. No. 10 of the *Keynotes* series, cover and title page designed by Aubrey Beardsley. (Contains 'The Bohemian Girl,' 'Mercedes,' 'A Broken Looking-Glass,' 'The Reward of Virtue,' 'A Re-incarnation,' 'Flower O' the Quince,' 'When I Am King,' 'A Responsibility' and 'Castles Near Spain').

12a — Boston, Robert Bros., London, John Lane, 1895.*

13 *Comedies and Errors.* London & New York, John Lane, 1898. (Contains 'The Confidante,' 'Merely Players,' 'The Friend of Man,' 'Tirala-Tirala,' 'The Invisible Prince,' 'P'tit Bleu,' 'The House of Eulalie,' 'The Queen's Pleasure,' 'Cousin Rosalys,' 'Flower O' the Clove,' 'Rooms' and 'Rosemary for Remembrance').

14 *The Cardinal's Snuff-Box.* London & New York, John Lane, 1900.

14a — New York, American News Co., [1900].*

14b — New York, American News Co., [1900]. *The People's Library* series.*

14c — New York, Grosset & Dunlap, (1900).*

14d — Leipzig, Tauchnitz, 1903. *Collection of British Authors*, Vol. No. 3671.

14e — Illustrated by G. C. Wilmshurst, London & New York, John Lane, 1903.

14f — Illustrated by F. H. Townsend, London, Newnes, (1904). *Newnes Sixpenny Novels Illustrated* series.

14g — Frontispiece by Dudley Tennant. London & Edinburgh, Nelson (1912). *The Nelson Library* series.

14h — New York, Dodd, Mead & Co., 1927.*

14i — Harmondsworth & New York, Penguin Books, 1946. *Penguin Books*, Vol. No. 580.

15 *The Lady Paramount.* London, John Lane, 1902.

15a — New York, John Lane, 1902. Copyright edition.*

15b — London & New York, John Lane, 1902.

15c — New York, Dodd, Mead & Co. and London, John Lane, (1902).*

15d — Leipzig, Tauchnitz, 1903. *Collection of British Authors*, Vol. No. 3688.

15e — Illustrated by F. H. Townsend, London, Newnes, (1905). *Newnes' Sixpenny Novels Illustrated* series.

16 *My Friend Prospero.* (New York) McClure, (1903). Advance copy for

private circulation only. (Serialized in *McClure's Magazine*, June-November, 1903).*

16a — Frontispiece by Louis Loeb. New York, McClure, Phillips & Co., 1904.

16b — London & New York, Bodley Head, 1904.*

16c — London & New York, John Lane, 1904.*

16d — Frontispiece by Louis Loeb. Toronto, Briggs, 1904.

16e — Leipzig, Tauchnitz, 1904. *Collection of British Authors*, Vol.No. 3725.

16f — New York, Wessels, (1904).*

16g — Illustrated by E. J. Sullivan. London, Newnes, (1906). *Newnes' Sixpenny Novels Illustrated* series.

16h — Frontispiece by J. R. Skelton. London, Nelson, (1913). *The Nelson Library* series.

16i — Harmondsworth & New York, Penguin Books, 1947. *Penguin Books* Vol. No. 596.

17 *The Royal End*. London, Hutchinson, 1909 (Published posthumously; completed by Aline Harland).

17a — New York, Dodd, Mead & Co., 1909.

17b — Leipzig, Tauchnitz, 1909. *Collection of British Authors*, Vol. No. 4104.

17c — Frontispiece by (Hilda Gargett?), London, Hutchinson, 1911. Foreword by Aline Harland.

18 *The Light Sovereign* (with Hubert Crackanthorpe). London, Lady Henry Harland, (1917).

II Uncollected Writings of Henry Harland

[Harland published an unknown number of short stories and 'literary letters' in American newspapers during the 1880s, which remain unidentified.]

'A Purim Episode.'[1] *Jewish Messenger* (New York), December 11, 1885, p. 9.

'The Story of Angela.'[1] *Lippincott's Monthly Magazine* (Philadelphia), January, 1887, pp. 85-119.

'The King's Touch.' *Liber Scriptorum*. New York: Authors Club, 1893, pp. 173-5. [Harland's only published poem.]

'A Duel.' *The Idler*, March, 1894, pp. 184-92.

'Bibi.' *English Illustrated Magazine*, April, 1894, pp. 725-31.

'A Letter to the Editor and an Offer of a Prize from the "Yellow Dwarf." ' *Yellow Book*, October, 1895, pp. 125-43.

'A Birthday Letter from the "Yellow Dwarf." ' *Yellow Book*, April, 1896, pp. 11-22.

'Dogs, Cats, Books and the Average Man by the "Yellow Dwarf": A Letter to the Editor.' *Yellow Book*, July, 1896, pp. 11-23.

'O.S.' *The Academy*, April 24, 1897, pp. 453-4. [A discussion of Owen Seaman's verse occasioned by the appearance of *The Battle of the Bays*.]

'Concerning the Short Story.' *The Academy*, June 5, 1897, Academy Fiction Supplement, pp. 6-7.

'Madame Guilbert.' *Literature*, July 4, 1898, pp. 645-7.

A Neighbourly Suggestion.' *The Academy*, October 22, 1898, p. 124.

'Mr Henry James.' *The Academy*, November 26, 1898, pp. 339-40.
'Aubrey Beardsley.' *The Academy*, December 10, 1898, pp. 437-8.
'Introduction' to Octave Feuillet's *The Romance of a Poor Young Man*, trans.
C. G. Compton. London: William Heinemann; New York: D. Appleton, 1902.

III The Correspondence of Henry and Aline Harland. [The count includes transcripts as well as autograph letters and post cards written by Henry Harland (HH) and Aline Harland (AH).]

Boston Public Library	HH: 14.		
Boston University	HH: 1.		
Brigham Young University	HH: 1.		
Cambridge University	HH: 2.		
Columbia University	HH: 53;	AH: 39.	
Connecticut College		AH: 10.	
Folger Shakespeare Library	HH: 1.		
Free Library of Philadelphia	HH: 1.		
Harvard University	HH: 14.		
Historical Society of Pennsylvania	HH: 1.		
Library of Congress	HH: 11.		
Loyola University (Chicago)	HH: 10.		
New York Public Library (Berg Coll.)	HH: 17;	AH: 4.	
New York Public Library (MS. Div.)	HH: 1;	AH: 3.	
New York University	HH: 2.		
Oxford University (Bodleian Library)	HH: 2;	AH: 1.	
Oxford University (Merton College)		AH: 1.	
Pennsylvania State University	HH: 2.		
Princeton University	HH: 4.		
Rochester University	HH: 1.		
Rutgers University	HH: 13.		
Stanford University		AH: 15.	
University of California (Los Angeles)	HH: 3.		
University of Leeds		AH: 2.	
University of Southern California	HH: 1.		
University of Texas (Austin)	HH: 11.		
University of Virginia	HH: 3.		
Westfield College, University of London	HH: 52;	AH: 16.	
Yale University	HH: 3.		

IV Additional Unpublished Sources

Clarke, John J. 'Henry Harland: A Critical Biography.' Unpub. doctoral dissertation, Brown University, 1957. [Good on secondary sources but makes no use of unpublished Harland correspondence.]
Fuller, Margaret. Letters. Connecticut College and Stanford University.
Harland, Mrs Thomas. Letters. Connecticut College and Stanford University.
Howe, Louise. Notes on Henry Harland and Letters. Stanford University.
Roberts, Donald A. 'Henry Harland: The Luska Phase.' Unpub. M.A. thesis, Columbia University, 1928.

Stedman, Edmund Clarence. Papers and Diaries. Columbia University.
Stedman, Laura. Notes on Henry Harland. Columbia University.

V Select General Bibliography

Annual Catalogue of Adelphi Academy (Brooklyn), 1871-5.
Baring, Maurice. *The Puppet Show of Memory*. London: Heinemann, 1922.
Beardsley, Aubrey. *The Letters of Aubrey Beardsley*, ed. Henry Maas, J. L.
    Duncan, and W. G. Good. London: Cassell & Co., 1970.
Beerbohm, Max. *Letters to Reggie*, ed. Rupert Hart-Davis. London: Rupert
    Hart-Davis, 1964.
—. *Seven Men*. London: Heinemann, 1919.
Benkovitz, Miriam. *Frederick Rolfe, Baron Corvo: A Biography*. London:
    Hamish Hamilton, 1977.
Brooks, Van Wyck. *The Confident Years: 1885-1915*. New York: Dutton, 1952.
Brown, E. K. *Willa Cather: A Critical Biography*. Completed by Leon Edel.
    New York: Alfred A. Knopf, 1953.
Burke, Rev. John J. 'Mr Henry Harland's Novels.' *Catholic World* (New
    York), June, 1902, pp. 398-403.
Carpenter, William H. 'The Editor of the "Yellow Book." ' *The Bookman*
    (New York), March, 1895, pp. 87-8.
Chalmers, Patrick. *Kenneth Grahame*. London: Methuen, 1933.
Charteris, Evan. *John Sargent*. London: Heinemann, 1927.
Cheshire, David and Malcolm Bradbury. 'American Realism and the Romance
    of Europe: Fuller, Frederic, Harland.' *Perspectives in American History*.
    Vol. IV. Cambridge, Mass.: Charles Warren Center for Studies in
    American History, Harvard University, 1970, pp. 285-310.
'The Church in Fiction.' *Catholic Book Notes*, June 10, 1904, p. 163. [Rev. of
    My Friend Prospero.]
C[okayne], G. E., ed. *Complete Baronetage*. Exeter: William Pollard & Co.,
    1906.
Edel, Leon, *Henry James: The Master, 1901-1916*. London: Rupert Hart-
    Davis, 1972.
Egerton, George. *A Leaf from the Yellow Book: The Correspondence of George
    Egerton*, ed. Terence de Vere White. London: Richards Press, 1958.
Elwin, Malcolm. *Old Gods Falling*. London: Collins, 1939.
Fuller, Margaret. *A New England Childhood*. Boston: Little, Brown & Co.,
    1916.
Gilcher, Edwin. *Bibliography of George Moore*. DeKalb, Ill.: Northern Illinois
    University Press, 1970.
Glastonbury, G. [Aline Harland] 'The Life and Writings of Henry Harland.'
    Irish Monthly, April, 1911, pp. 210-19.
Gosse, Edmund. 'A First Sight of Verlaine.' *The Savoy*, April, 1896, pp.
    113-6; rpt. in *French Profiles* (London, 1905).
'A Half-Score New Novelists.' *Atlantic Monthly* (Boston), February, 1886,
    pp. 260-1.
Harkins, F. E. *Little Pilgrimages Among the Men Who Have Written Famous
    Books*. Second Series. Boston: L. C. Page & Co., 1903.

[Harris, Frank]. 'Three Yellow Book Story-Tellers.' *Saturday Review*, June 1, 1895, pp. 730-1.

Henderson, Archibald. 'Recent Novels of Note.' *Sewanee Review* (Sewanee, Tenn.), October, 1904, pp. 456-8.

'Henry Harland (Sidney Luska), 1861-1905.' *Bibliography of American Literature*. Vol. III. Ed. Jacob Blanck. New Haven: Yale University Press, 1959, pp. 377-83.

Hind, C. Lewis. *Naphtali*. London: John Lane, 1926.

[Howells, William Dean.] 'Editor's Study.' *Harper's New Monthly Magazine* (New York), May, 1889, p. 987. [Rev. of *A Latin-Quarter Courtship* and *Grandison Mather*.]

—. 'Editor's Study.' *Harper's New Monthly Magazine*, July, 1886, pp. 314-5. [Rev. of *Mrs Peixada*.]

—. *Life in Letters of William Dean Howells*. 2 vols. Ed. Mildred Howells. Garden City, N.Y.: Doubleday, 1928.

Hoyt, Eleanor. 'Current Fiction.' *The Lamp* (New York), March, 1904, pp. 154-5. [Rev. of *My Friend Prospero*.]

Huntley, John. 'Aline and Henry Harland, Aubrey Beardsley, and "The Yellow Book": A Verification of Some Evidence.' *Notes and Queries*, March, 1962, pp. 107-8.

James, Henry. *Letters of Henry James*. 2 vols. Ed. Percy Lubbock. New York. Charles Scribner's Sons, 1920.

—. 'Preface' to Vol. XV, *The Novels and Tales of Henry James*. New York: Charles Scribner's Sons, 1909.

—. 'The Story-Teller at Large: Mr Henry Harland.' *Fortnightly Review*, April 1, 1898, pp. 650-4.

Kitcat, Mabel. 'Henry Harland in London.' *The Bookman* (New York), August, 1909, pp. 609-13. [Excerpts from letters.]

Kobbé, Gustave. 'Timely Interviews.' *The Lamp* (New York), April, 1903, pp. 225-6.

Lane, John. *Aubrey Beardsley and the Yellow Book*. London & New York: John Lane, 1903.

Le Gallienne, Richard. *Retrospective Reviews: A Literary Log*. 2 vols. London: John Lane; New York: Dodd, Mead, 1896.

—. *Robert Louis Stevenson: An Elegy and Other Poems*. London: John Lane; New York: Copeland & Day, 1895.

—. *The Romantic '90s*. London: Putnam & Co., 1951.

'Lounger.' Comment on Harland as the 'Yellow Dwarf.' *The Critic* (New York), January 9, 1897, p. 27.

—. Comment on Harland's failure to copyright *The Cardinal's Snuff-Box* in America. *The Critic*, April, 1902, p. 306.

MacColl, D. S. 'Memories of the Nineties.' *London Mercury*, January, 1939, pp. 287-96.

MacDonald, George E. *Fifty Years of Free-Thought*. 2 vols. New York: The Truth Seeker Co., 1929.

Mattheisen, Paul F. and Michael Millgate, eds. *Transatlantic Dialogue: Selected American Correspondence of Edmund Gosse*. Austin, Texas & London: University of Texas Press, 1965.

Maurice, Arthur B. *New York in Fiction.* New York: Dodd, Mead & Co., 1901.

May, J. Lewis. *John Lane and the Nineties.* London: John Lane, 1936.

Mayne, Ethel Colburn. *Browning's Heroines.* London: Chatto & Windus, 1913.

McClure, S.S. *My Autobiography.* London: John Murray, 1914.

Meynell, Viola. *Alice Meynell.* London: Jonathan Cape, 1929.

Mix, Katherine L. *A Study in Yellow: The Yellow Book and its Contributors.* Lawrence, Kansas & London: University of Kansas Press, 1960.

Moore, George. *Confessions of a Young Man,* ed. Susan Dick. Montreal & London: McGill – Queen's University Press, 1972.

'Mr Henry Harland.' *New York Herald,* December 13, 1903, Third Section, pp. 4-5.

Nelson, James G. *The Early Nineties: A View from the Bodley Head.* Cambridge, Mass.: Harvard University Press, 1971.

'Notes About Authors.' *The Book-Buyer* (New York), January, 1886, p. 395. [Harland's identity revealed.]

Obituary of Edward Harland. *Norwich Bulletin,* March 10, 1915, p. 5.

Obituary of Henry Harland. *The Athenaeum,* December 30, 1905, p. 898.

Obituary of Henry Harland. *The Times* (London), December 22, 1905, p. 10.

Obituary of Henry Harland. *The World* (New York), December 22, 1905, p. 9.

Obituary of Mrs Thomas Harland. *Norwich Bulletin,* January 21, 1925, p. 5.

Obituary of Thomas Harland. *New York Daily Tribune,* April 27, 1900, p. 7.

O'Brien, Justin. 'Henry Harland, An American Forerunner of Proust.' *Modern Language Notes* (Baltimore), June, 1939, pp. 420-8.

'On the Writing of Novels.' *The Critic* (New York), March 24, 1888, p. 137. [Harland's letter concerning the creative process.]

'Open Letter to the Author of *The Yoke of the Thorah.' The Jewish Messenger* (New York), July 22, 1887, p. 1. [Signed by 'Cyril.']

O'Sullivan, Vincent. *Opinions.* London: Unicorn Press, 1959.

Our Own Times.' *The Reader* (Indianapolis), September, 1906, p. 442. [An account of Harland's life.]

Parry, Albert. *Garrets and Pretenders: A History of Bohemianism in America.* New York: Covici-Friede, 1933.

—. 'Henry Harland: Expatriate.' *The Bookman* (New York), January, 1933, pp. 1-10.

Pater, Walter. *Letters of Walter Pater,* ed. Lawrence Evans. Oxford: Oxford University Press, 1970.

Patmore, Derek. *Portrait of My Family.* London: Cassell & Co., 1935.

Pennell, Elizabeth Robins. *The Life and Letters of Joseph Pennell.* 2 vols. Boston: Little, Brown & Co., 1929.

—. *Nights: Rome and Venice in the Aesthetic Eighties, London and Paris in the Fighting Nineties.* Philadelphia & London: J. B. Lippincott, 1916.

Pope, Charles H., comp. *Merriam Genealogy in England and America.* Boston: C. H. Pope, 1906.

'Popularity.' *The Academy,* May 3, 1902, pp. 459-60. [Rev. of *The Lady Paramount.*]

Rev. of *As It Was Written. Jewish Messenger* (New York), September 25,

1885, p. 5; *New York Daily Tribune*, September 22, 1885, p. 6; *New York Times*, October 5, 1885, p. 2.

Rev. of *Latin-Quarter Courtship*. *The Critic* (New York), May 11, 1889, p. 233.

Rev. of *Mea Culpa*. *The Athenaeum*, May 16, 1891, p. 632.

Rev. of *Mrs Peixada*. *The Critic* (New York), April 10, 1886, p. 180; *New York Times*, April 5, 1886, p. 3.

Rev. of *Yellow Book*, Vol. XII. *The Times*, January 29, 1897, p. 14.

Richards, John M. *The Life of John Oliver Hobbes*. London: John Murray, 1911.

Roberts, Donald A. 'Henry Harland and His World.' *Commonweal* (New York), February 8, 1928, pp. 1039-40.

—. 'Henry Harland, '82 – College Years.' *City College Alumnus* (New York), February-March, 1930, pp. 23-4.

[Rolfe, Frederick], Baron Corvo. *Letters to Grant Richards*. St. Ives: Peacocks Press, 1952.

—. *Nicholas Crabbe; or The One and the Many*. London: Chatto & Windus, 1958.

—. *Without Prejudice: One Hundred Letters to John Lane*, ed. Cecil Woolf. London: Privately Printed, 1963.

Ross, Margery, ed. *Robert Ross: Friend of Friends*. London: Jonathan Cape, 1952.

Sharp, Evelyn. *Unfinished Adventure*. London: John Lane, 1933.

Sharp, William. 'New Novels.' *The Academy*, November 30, 1889, p. 352. [Rev. of *Grandison Mather*.]

Stedman, Arthur. 'An American Author Abroad.' *Philadelphia Press*, August 5, 1894, p. 28.

Stedman, Laura and George M. Gould. *Life and Letters of Edmund Clarence Stedman*. 2 vols. New York: Moffat, Yard & Co., 1910.

Symons, Arthur. 'Literary Causerie: By Way of Epilogue.' *The Savoy*, No. 8 (December, 1896), pp. 91-2.

—. *The Memoirs of Arthur Symons: Life and Art in the 1890s*, ed. Karl Beckson. University Park, Pa. & London: Pennsylvania State University Press, 1977.

Syrett, Netta. *The Sheltering Tree*. London: Geoffrey Bles, 1939.

Thornton, Alfred. 'Diary of an Art Student of the Nineties.' *The Artist*, April-May, 1935, pp. 53-4; pp. 86-7.

Tindall, William York. *Forces in Modern British Literature, 1885-1956*. New York: Vintage Books, 1956.

Waugh, Arthur. 'London Letter.' *The Critic* (New York), January 20, 1894, pp. 42-44; April 24, 1894, p. 290; May 5, 1894, p. 312; November 30, 1895, p. 374.

—. *One Man's Road*. London: Chapman & Hall, 1931.

Weeks, Donald. *Corvo*. London: Michael Joseph, 1971.

Weintraub, Stanley. *Aubrey Beardsley: Imp of the Perverse*. University Park, Pa. & London: Pennsylvania State University Press, 1976.

'What the "Yellow Book" Is To Be.' *The Sketch*, April 11, 1894, pp. 557-8. [An interview with Harland and Beardsley.]

Whyte, Frederick. *A Bachelor's London*. London: Grant Richards, 1931.
Wilde, Oscar. 'The Critic as Artist.' *Complete Works of Oscar Wilde*, ed.
    J. B. Foreman. London: Collins, 1970.
—. *Letters of Oscar Wilde*, ed. Rupert Hart-Davis. London: Rupert Hart-
    Davis, 1962.
Yeats, W. B. *Autobiographies*, London: Macmillan, 1926.
'A Yellow Bore.' *The Critic* (New York), November 10, 1894, p. 316. [Rev.
    of the *Yellow Book*, Vol. III.]
'A Yellow Melancholy.' *The Speaker*, April 28, 1894, pp. 468-9. [Rev. of the
    Yellow Book, Vol. I.]

Index

111, 112, 117, 120, 123, 124,
127-31, 132-39, 140, 144, 145,
146, 147, 149, 150, 151, 152;
letters to: Richard W. Gilder,
133-34;
Edmund Gosse, 130-31;
Mrs Irene Harland and Edward
Harland, 136;
Louise Howe, 135, 136, 137;
E. C. Stedman, 43-44, 53, 54, 64-
65, 68, 73, 127-28, 132-33;
Mrs E. C. Stedman, 49;
'G. Glastonbury' (pseudonym),
'The Life and Writings of Henry
Harland,' 140, 141, 142, 144,
145, 148, 149, 151;
trans., Serao's *Farewell, Love*, 144
Harland, Caroline Ruth (sister), 141
Harland, Gen. Edward (uncle), 2,
3, 4, 7, 123, 135, 151, 152
Harland, Henry
accused of anti-Semitism, 30-32
adoption of pseudonym, 15-16
and the Aesthetic Movement, 10,
98, 109
alleged pseudonym of 'Robert
Shews,' 148-49
birthplace, 2, 94, 140
at City College, 6-8, 9, 94
claim to a baronetcy, 88, 121, 136
conversion to Roman Catholicism,
108-9
on the creative process, 35, 66,
105-6
early schooling, 5
earnings from writings, 25, 62,
105, 116, 150-51
on England, 97, 120, 124, 125
family background, 2
on fiction, 50, 52
on France, 75-76, 97, 113
friendships and professional,
relationships: Aubrey Beardsley,
56-59, 66-67, 69-70, 71, 80-81,
109;
Witter Bynner, 2, 123-25, 140;
Olive Custance, 89-98;
Ella D'Arcy, 60-61;

Edmund Gosse, 47, 48, 49,
50-51, 59, 115, 118-20;
William Dean Howells, 33-34,
35, 41-42, 128;
Henry James, 78, 83, 106-7,
107-8;
John Lane, 54, 56-57, 58-59,
61-62, 67, 71, 74, 84-85, 87,
88, 105, 106, 150;
Richard Le Gallienne, 66, 75-
76;
Samuel S. McClure, 22-24, 129;
D. S. MacColl, 53, 54, 55, 56;
Frederick Rolfe('Baron Corvo'),
85, 109-12;
E. C. Stedman, 1, 8, 10, 14-17,
22-24, 27-29, 35-36, 40, 41, 42,
43, 48, 52, 132;
Oscar Wilde, 65, 148
at Harvard, 8-10, 141
health, 48, 49-50, 103, 107, 119,
125, 128-30
influence of Felix Adler, 6
interest in Jews, 6, 15, 33
on Jews, 21, 26, 33, 88, 113-14,
117-18, 121, 126, 134
letters to: Witter Bynner, 124;
Frederick Chapman, 81, 116;
Olive Custance, 90-94, 97;
Dr. Richard Garnett, 60;
Edmund Gosse, 49, 51-52, 81,
107, 108, 113, 115-16, 118-19;
William Dean Howells, 32,
33-34, 41-42, 44;
Mrs W. D. Howells, 37;
Jewish Messenger, 31-32;
John Lane, 60, 61-62, 66, 67,
71, 73, 74, 80, 84-85, 105, 113,
114-15, 149, 150;
Richard Le Gallienne, 60, 66,
75, 76, 83;
Samuel S. McClure, 22-3;
Frederick Rolfe ('Baron Corvo')
112;
E. C. Stedman, 14-15, 23-24,
27, 28-29, 39, 41, 43, 48-49,
50, 52, 53, 142;
T. Fisher Unwin, 46-47;